for

Father Bob

who inspired, encouraged and supported

my efforts

to seek out

new ways of expressing

my spirituality

and faith in God

ANNUNCIATION

†

INCARNATION

†

MANIFESTATION

Advent to Epiphany Meditations

Diane Zike

Foolscap & Quill

ISBN 978-0-9718552-7-4

ISBN 978-1-938143-18-2

UPC 8-03236-700078

Published by:
Foolscap & Quill, LLC
P. O. Box 1018
Morrison, CO 80465-1018
www.foolscap-quill.com

FORWARD

Annunciation, Incarnation and Manifestation

The three words that make up the title of these meditations provide the connections between the seasons of Advent, Christmas and Epiphany. They are also links to the major theme of the seasons: the son of God coming into the world. The conception of Jesus is announced to Mary. "The Holy Spirit will come upon you, and the power of the Most High will overshadow you; therefore the child to be born will be holy; he will be called Son of God." (Luke 1:35) God is born in human flesh at Christmas. "To you is born this day in the city of David a Saviour, who is the Messiah, the Lord." (Luke 2:11). The visit of the wise men is the introduction of the Christ child into the world. "Where is the child who has been born king of the Jews? For we observed his star at its rising, and have come to pay him homage." (Matthew 2:2)

I believe an important reason to have seasons of the church is to provide opportunities to focus on specific themes that inform our faith. Some themes like judgment and redemption are repeated in these meditations because they are major themes of the Advent and Christmas seasons. These three seasons together draw sharply into focus the fulfillment of God's promise to us in the birth of Jesus Christ our Redeemer.

ᘓ

Inspired by the Word and the World

I have been asked, "Why write meditations?" Every word or phrase I have used as a title or subject in these meditations spoke to me in some way. They may have jogged a memory or led me to some serious bible study. That's what I believe meditation is about —going where the Word of God takes you, and letting the Spirit be your guide.

I do prepare by reading the lessons, as well as other Bible passages, other meditations, books, and whatever I think will inspire me. As I read the lessons I wait for inspiration and am often caught off guard by thoughts forming on paper that were not where I thought I was going at all. Then I just try to go with the flow. Sometimes the title comes first, sometimes, surprisingly, the end comes first, and I am left to fill in the blank space.

I also want my work to reflect the world around me, to touch on things that move other people as well as move me. I look to the beauty of God's creation to inspire me and the harsh realities of life to get my attention. I want to celebrate the glory of God's creation and his love for us. But I also want to examine how and why we struggle to fulfill God's will for us.

I am blessed and humbled by a gift that moves me not only to create images of life, but also to share those images with others. I share how I see the Word of God reflected in the world and I share how I see the world reflected in the Word of God. My hope and my prayer is that the words and thoughts that I have shared with you for these holy seasons of the church will inform and inspire you as well.

Let the words of my mouth and the meditation of my heart
be acceptable to you,
O Lord, my rock and my redeemer.

Psalm 19:14

Thank you, Lord, for the gift of words. May I always use them to speak your truth and glorify your name. *Amen.*

Note: These meditations use the lessons from the Revised Common Lectionary (Year B-2). The daily lessons are used with exception of Sundays, Christmas Eve, Christmas, Stephen, St. John, the Holy Innocents, Eve of the Holy Name, Holy Name of Jesus, Eve of the Epiphany, and Epiphany. The readings for the day are noted at the bottom of the page and the reading(s) used are highlighted.

II

Advent 1

You are my son; today I have begotten you.

Psalm 2:7

Sunday   First Sunday of Advent

Tear Open the Heavens

O that you would tear open the heavens
and come down.

Isaiah 64:1

Isn't that what we really want? Don't we want a God who is Superman; a God who will swoop down and wipe out all our enemies and solve all our problems? He would rule the world from his throne on high, and we would be able to sit back and relax, knowing that God is taking care of everything for us. Wow, what a Christmas present that would be!

The Israelites had similar expectations of a God who would come down into the world like a mighty warrior "so that the mountains would quake at your presence." (vs. 1) The Old Testament authors described an almighty and powerful God. The Savior God promised to send would destroy the enemies of the Jewish people.

The Savior that God did send to the Israelites, and to us, was someone very different. We usually think of that difference in terms of a helpless infant laying in a manger rather than a mighty king upon a throne. We think of a baby born in modest surroundings rather than someone famous and wealthy surrounded by all the trappings of royalty. There was a lot more to the difference between Jesus and the world's expectations of God-made-man.

Think for a minute about what the Bible tells us about Jesus; what he was really like. The boy Jesus was a good kid —most of the time. "The child grew and became strong, filled with wisdom; and the favour of God was upon him." (Luke 2:40) There was at least one time when he got in a bit of trouble, lagging behind at the temple. He sounded like a pretty typical twelve year old

3

when he asked his parents, "Why were you searching for me?" (Luke 2:49).

Jesus probably trained to be a carpenter like Joseph but he seems to have spent most of his adult life as an itinerate preacher. He traveled around the countryside curing sick people, preaching and praying. Jesus liked having little children around and he spent a lot of time with his friends, but he made some people uncomfortable because he also befriended tax collectors and the unclean. He didn't always follow the rules of the Jewish society

Jesus may have started out as simply a helpless baby but he seemed to have turned out to be quite a wonderful person. He was someone you would have wanted to have for a neighbor or a friend. This God-made-man was truly God and truly human, incorporating all that was supernatural about God and all that was natural about a human being. No, Jesus never became an earthly king, but he was God and man, and so much more.

Jesus, you took on human life, you chose to walk among us. Now we have had a small glimpse of the love and compassion of God. You have led us and guided us in ways no earthly king could do. Your gift to us could not be matched by all of the celebrations of your coming into the world; you gave your life for us. Help me to prepare my heart for your coming and to prepare my spirit to welcome you home.

Heavenly Father, we have been told that Jesus will come some day in all his glory to be among us again as the true ruler of the world. Tear open the heavens and let Jesus come down into our lives again! We await him with open arms and hearts. Welcome, brother and friend. *Amen.*

Psalm 80:1-7, 16-18;
Isaiah 64:1-9; 1 Corinthians 1:3-9; Mark 13(24-37)

Monday   Week of Advent 1

The Son of God

You are my son; today I have begotten you.

Psalm 2:7

The primary focus of Advent is on the coming of Jesus into the world, the beginning of life on earth of our Savior. Advent also marks the beginning of the church year, and appropriately the readings for Advent begin with the first three psalms. In Psalm 2 God sets the theme for the season: "You are my son; today I have begotten you." (Psalm 2:7). Here, in the Old Testament God declares his special relationship with his son and on Sundays and other major feast days we commemorate God's witness to his son when we recite the Nicene Creed. "We believe in our Lord, Jesus Christ, the only Son of God, eternally begotten of the Father." (*Book of Common Prayer*, 358) In Advent we prepare for the birth of this special son of God.

Even though it was revealed to both Mary and Joseph that the baby Jesus was the Son of God, the savior of the Jewish people, they made no special plans for his birth. In fact, they were away from home, taking part in a census ordered by the Roman authorities. This son of God was born in a stable "because there was no room for them in the inn." (Luke 2:7).

To us it might seem odd that God made no special preparations for the birth of his son. God could easily have made sure that the birth of Jesus was met with great fanfare and celebration. He could have at least made sure that Mary was at home, surrounded by family and friends when she gave birth.

The life of Jesus certainly began with some unusual events. The night of his birth an angel appeared to shepherds and told them that the Messiah had been born. "To you is born this day in the city of David a Saviour, who is the Messiah, the Lord." (Luke 2:11) Then three wise men sought out the Christ Child, declaring him "born king of the Jews." (Matthew 2:2) and bringing him gifts. These were the ways God chose to announce the birth of his son.

We do celebrate the birth of a new child with announcements just as the angels announced the birth of Jesus to the shepherds. And we do bring gifts for a new baby. However, many of the preparations for the remembrance of the birth of Jesus are more like those for the celebration of a birthday. And indeed Christmas is a birth-day celebration.

The beginning of the life of Jesus is a very special time in our lives. Jesus is bringing his own special gift to us. He is bringing us salvation. Advent is a time of preparation for the beginning of our promised new life in Christ. It is a very special time, celebrating a very special birth. We need to prepare; we need to celebrate.

Father, we thank you for the gift of your son. May our Advent preparations and our Christmas celebrations always reflect the special meaning of the birth of your son as fulfillment of your promise of redemption. *Amen.*

AM: *Psalm* 1, *2*, 3; PM: Psalm 4, 7;
Amos 2:6-16; 2 Peter 1:1-11; Matthew 21:1-11

6

Tuesday   Week of Advent 1

The Fig Tree

'May no fruit ever come from you again!' And the fig tree withered at once.

Matthew 21:19

"May no fruit come from you ever again." I am sure that, I too would have withered "at once" if Jesus directed these words to me; I cringe just reading these words! This seems like the harshest of judgments coming from our Lord! What had that poor little fig tree done to deserve the wrath of God?

A simple answer is that Jesus was seeking fruit from the fig tree and the tree was not bearing any fruit. And that is the purpose of a fruit tree. We are like that fig tree. We have a purpose, and our purpose is also to bear fruit. Our fruit is not figs or apples. Each one of us has a purpose as a child of God and our lives are meant to bear forth the fruit of that purpose just as the fig tree's purpose is to bear figs.

Anticipation of the celebration of the birth of Christ brings to mind the fruits of the life of Jesus. The purpose of Jesus' life was to do the will of the Father: "I glorified you on earth by finishing the work that you gave me to do.... I have made your name known to those whom you gave me from the world." (John 17: 4-6) Jesus assumed human form to help people know God, and to be the perfect sacrifice for the sins of the whole world. Jesus' offering of himself was the fruit he offered to the Father, the fulfillment of his purpose.

Jesus used the example of bearing fruit earlier in the gospel of John when he referred to himself as the true vine. "I am the vine, you are the branches. Those who abide in me and I in them bear much fruit, because apart from me you can do nothing." (John 15:5) Jesus knew that if he was not "alive" in the disciples they could bear no fruit. We also cannot bear fruit if Christ is not alive in us.

Sometimes the words of Jesus do seem harsh, but they are meant to teach us. He uses examples such as the fig tree and the grape vine to show how we are to lead our lives as a reflection of his life. We could not survive without the love of Jesus just as a fig tree or a grapevine could not survive without good soil, water and sunshine. When these elements are present in nature plants thrive; without them they cannot bear fruit, and the plants may wither or even die.

When our lives become a reflection of the life and love of Christ, we bear the fruits of faith and righteousness. Then our purpose is fulfilled and we glorify the Father just as Jesus glorified the Father by his works on earth. Jesus lives in us and us in him just as Jesus is in the Father and the Father in him.

Blessed Jesus, May your words and example always teach us how to live godly lives in your name. Be for us the true vine so that we can bear much fruit. Please accept the humble offering of the fruits of our lives as our gift of love for you and our heavenly Father. *Amen.*

AM: Psalm 5, 6; PM: Psalm 10, 11;
Amos 3:1-11; 2 Peter 1:12-21; *Matthew 21:12-22*

Wednesday   Week of Advent 1

All Are Punish'd

I will tear down the winter house as well as the
summer house;
  and the houses of ivory shall perish,
  and the great houses shall come to an end

Amos 3:15

When I read this passage I wanted to shout: "Go God!" It was a bad week. The news of the rich and powerful, the greedy and the arrogant had been unrelenting. There were stories about some shady bankers who hired people to forge banking executives' signatures on mortgage documents so they could fleece the helpless faster. Some banks also somehow conveniently "lost" mortgage papers and then those papers magically reappeared in time for foreclosure.

I read the story of a very wealthy woman who liked to use her wealth to "rescue" her famous pals who got into trouble. But she had fallen on "hard" times. Unfortunately she had taken the advice of a friend and lost a lot of money to a scheming man who had fleeced her and many others and was now behind bars. This dear lady was in a bit of a bind. She was living on her "equity," on the value of the five or so mansions she still owned. Many people have no equity left thanks to the greed of a few.

These stories had come fast on the heels of the great congressional budget battle where promises and politics were obviously more important than compromise and shared sacrifices. It was somehow more important to protect the tax shelters of the rich than to insure that people had jobs and food.

9

I would gladly have rooted God on as he tore down the mansions of the rich. I wanted to see those "who oppress the poor, who crush the needy," brought down low for their selfishness. I was ready for God to wreak havoc, to have his revenge.

Then an inevitable but feared moment came. The credit rating of the great United States was lowered. How could this be? The thought that the mighty United States could be less than perfect sent stock markets tumbling and had the politicians falling all over themselves to pin the blame any place but with themselves. We, the people, looked on in horror and said to one another, "What have *they* done?"

This was as much of a wake-up call as the pronouncements and the dire warnings of the prophet Amos. Most people have been hurt in some way by the current financial difficulties of our country. As the Prince in Romeo and Juliet said to the feuding families who had lost their heirs to their selfishness, "all are punish'd." (*Romeo and Juliet*, William Shakespeare, Act V, Scene III, 295). Unfortunately the suffering is not proportional. It may be difficult to lose a lot of money; it is a very different situation to lose your home, your job, your insurance.

Now is the time to get our financial house in order. We need to find a way to work together to get through these hard times; we must make hard choices and changes. And we need to come up with a fair way for all to share the burden. We must find just and compassionate means to move from our chaotic times to a world where there is a more equitable sharing of wealth and resources.

Lord, we deserve just punishment for our sin and folly. Please treat us with mercy and grant us grace to lead new lives of compassion and caring that will reflect your love. *Amen.*

AM: Psalm 119:1-24; PM: Psalm 12, 13, 14;
Amos 3:12-4:5; 2 Pet. 3:1-10; Matthew 21:23-32

Thursday   Week of Advent 1

Judgment Day

And I also withheld the rain from you
  when there were still three months to the harvest;
I would send rain on one city,
  and send no rain on another city;
one field would be rained upon,
  and the field on which it did not rain withered

Amos 4:7

This passage really struck a chord with me as I read it on a blistering summer day in the middle of a severe drought. More than once in the past week storms had built up and some places had even experienced sprinkles or a brief shower, but our burnt-up lawns and limp flowers remained parched and dry, and voluntary rationing had begun in the city. As the temperatures soared under the unrelenting sun beating down, it was sad to watch many plants die, but it was much sadder to hear of so many people being taken to emergency rooms, and even some heat-related deaths.

I was so tired of watering every day, and I, like so many others was praying for rain. A friend mentioned to me in a phone conversation that afternoon that some storms were building out to the west. I responded that if we received rain she could find me dancing in the street.

As the sky grew darker and I could see the storm clouds approaching I ran from window to door — hoping, praying. No, I did not dance in the street, but as the rain poured down I grabbed every bucket, pot and container of every size I could find and filled them with wonderful, cool rain water, all the while thanking God for the glorious gift of rain. Later that evening the same friend called back to tell me their power was out, and they

11

had not had nearly as much rain as I had even though they only live a few miles from me.

Whether it is drought or flood; tornado or hurricane, we sometimes ask why one place is ravaged and another is not. Why are some blessed with rain and others left dry? Why are some spared and not others? Are some being judged or punished by God?

In this passage God does not explain why some are spared and others are not, but the chapter's refrain expresses God's displeasure with his people: "yet you did not return to me, says the Lord." For these people the day of judgment was at hand.

> *Therefore, thus I will do to you, O Israel;*
> *because I will do this to you,*
> *prepare to meet your God, O Israel!*
>
> Amos 4:12

We would do well to heed this message from the prophet Amos. Our attention should not be focused on who may have been punished or who may have been spared in earthly travails. We also would do well to remember that all will face a day of judgment before the Lord.

Lord, we know that some day we will stand before the throne of God on our own judgment day. Help us to heed your Word and follow the teachings of the prophets of our day as well as those in Holy Scripture so that we need not fear the wrath of God when that hour has come. *Amen.*

AM: Psalm 18:1-20; PM: Psalm 18:21-50;
Amos 4:6-13; 2 Pet. 3:11-18; Matthew 21:33-46

Friday   Week of Advent 1

Who is this God?

For I know how many are your transgressions,
and how great are your sins.

Amos 5:12

In today's lessons we have readings from both the Old and New Testament calling on the people to repent, warning of God's anger and wrathful punishment for disobedience. The prophet Amos pronounces God's displeasure. "For I know how many are your transgressions, and how great are your sins —you who afflict the righteous." (Amos 5:12) In The Letter of Jude the author reminds the evildoers of Enoch's prophecy of God's judgment. "See, the Lord is coming with tens of thousands of his holy ones, to execute judgment on all, and to convict everyone of all the deeds of ungodliness that they have committed in such an ungodly way, and of all the harsh things that ungodly sinners have spoken against him." (Jude 1:14-15)

Evolutionary biologist and avowed atheist Richard Dawkins has characterized the God of the Old Testament as a "monster." In a book he has written called *The God Delusion* Dawkins calls God "the most unpleasant character in all of fiction," and urges people to read the Old Testament and see for themselves. ("Darwin's Rottweiler," *Newsweek*, October 5, 2009, 54) That is not a bad idea but I would suggest that Dawkins needs to give the Old Testament a more careful examination. A closer look shows a God meting out both just punishment and mercy. In Genesis, after the Flood God makes a promise to Noah and his family: "I establish my covenant with you, that never again shall all flesh be cut off by the waters of a flood, and never again shall there be a flood to destroy the earth." (Genesis 9:11)

With more careful reading what some people, including

13

Dawkins, may discover is that these words of fury are usually spoken about God or for God. In other words, these pronouncements come from human lips, reflecting both the culture of the writers and a personal characterization of their God. Although these scriptures are considered to be the inspired word of God, in this written word he is a God seen through human eyes and depicted using human words. The writers of the Old Testament wrote about God as they experienced God in their time with their history, just as the authors of today write about God filtered through our own perspective and human history.

As Dawkins suggests we often look to the New Testament for a more loving and forgiving God. However, many times in the Old Testament God is persuaded not to carry out his threats of violence or vengeance. Here is an example from Amos:

> *The Lord God was calling for a shower of fire, and it devoured the great deep and was eating up the land. Then I said,*
> *'O Lord God, cease, I beg you!*
> *How can Jacob stand?*
> *He is so small!"*
> *The Lord relented concerning this;*
> *'This also shall not be,' said the Lord God.*
>
> (Amos 7:4-6)

God is a merciful and righteous judge. He loves those whom he has created, even though they sin against his will. Just consider the greatest second chance of all he gave to us. For once, for all time, for all — he gave his only begotten Son.

God, we characterize you as an angry, punishing God because we know that we have sinned against you and deserve punishment; we fear your anger and your wrath. Have mercy upon us. We pray for forgiveness of our sins so that we can see our God and ourselves from a new perspective: the light and love of the risen Christ. *Amen.*

AM: Psalm 16, 17; PM: Psalm 22;
Amos 5:1-17; Jude 1-16; Matthew 22:1-14

Saturday   Week of Advent 1

Jesus: Our Hearts' Desire

The Lord answer you in the day of trouble!

Psalm 20:1

"O Holy Night," a beautiful hymn of the Christmas season, tells of the plight of the world at the time of the birth of Jesus. The world had problems. God had answers.

O holy night! The stars are brightly shining,
It is the night of our dear Saviour's birth.
Long lay the world in sin and error pining
Till he appear'd and the soul felt its worth.

There was no way for the world to get itself out of its pit of sin and sorrow. Humankind had offended God and could not redeem itself. God knew that. And God loved the people he created. God gave to the world what he loved the most, his only son, to save the world from sin. "Now I know that the Lord will help his anointed; he will answer him from his holy heaven with mighty victories by his right hand." (Psalm 20:6)

People hoped and prayed for a Messiah as God had promised. When those prayers were answered the answer was not what people expected. Many expected a king or mighty warrior, but not a baby, born in a stable. How could a tiny baby save the world?

However, Jesus confounded the Israelites' expectations. He ministered to the outcast and the needy. He healed the sick and forgave the sinner. He preached love and peace, not division and war.

Jesus' victories were not over armies, but over slavery; mankind was enslaved by sin. Evil ruled the world.

Truly he taught us to love one another
His law is love and his gospel is peace.
Chains shall he break for the slave is our brother
And in his name all oppression shall cease.

God's answers to our pleas are not to fulfill our requests but to exceed our needs. He knows the deepest desires of our hearts. "May he grant you your heart's desire, and fulfill all your plans." (Psalm 20:4)

So humankind did not get what was wanted or expected but we received much, much more than we could ever have imagined. We were saved from our sins, not by any show of military might or regal decree, but by love. We were saved by the love God had for us and the love Jesus Christ showed for us.

Sweet hymns of joy in grateful chorus raise we,
Let all within us praise his holy name.
Christ is the Lord! O praise His Name forever,
His power and glory evermore proclaim.
His power and glory evermore proclaim.

"O Holy Night"
based on a poem by Placide Cappeau, 1847;
trans. by John Sullivan Dwight, 1855

Dear Jesus, you are the answer to all our prayers in your time, in our time, and forever more. *Amen.*

AM: **Psalm 20**, 21:1-7(8-14); PM: Psalm 110:1-5(6-7), 116, 117; Amos 5:18-27; Jude 17-25; Matthew 22:15-22

Advent 2

The beginning of the good news of Jesus Christ,
the Son of God.

Mark 1:1

Sunday   Second Sunday of Advent

The Beginning of the Good News

The beginning of the good news of Jesus Christ,
the Son of God.

Mark 1:1

All four gospels have decidedly different beginnings. The Gospel of Mark's introductory statement boldly declares it is, "the beginning of the good news of Jesus Christ." (Mark 1:1). The author also confesses his belief that Jesus is "the Son of God." In this prologue the "good news" is connected back to the Old Testament by the prophetic words of Isaiah and framed by the ministry of "John the baptizer."

Initially the focus was on John the Baptist as he traveled about in the wilderness, "proclaiming a baptism of repentance for the forgiveness of sins." (v. 4) John testified that a "more powerful one than I is coming after me." (v. 7) Jesus came to John to be baptized. "Now after John was arrested, Jesus came to Galilee, proclaiming the good news of God." (Mark 1:4-14) As the ministry of John the Baptist came to a close, the "good news," the ministry of Jesus began.

The Gospel of Matthew begins with the genealogy of Jesus, tracing his human roots as the "son of David, the son of Abraham... and Jacob the father of Joseph the husband of Mary, of whom Jesus was born," (Matthew 1:1-16). Matthew also introduces the divine connection of Jesus as "the Messiah."

Luke's gospel begins with an explanation for writing "an

19

orderly account... so that you may know the truth concerning the things about which you have been instructed." (Luke 1:3-4). Luke's story begins before the birth of Jesus, with an angel's announcement of the conception of John the Baptist. "But the angel said to him, 'Do not be afraid, Zechariah, for your prayer has been heard. Your wife Elizabeth will bear you a son, and you will name him John.'" (Luke 1:13)

The Gospel of John's beginning comes from a very different perspective, focusing not on the story of Jesus but on Jesus' relationship to God: "In the beginning was the Word, and the Word was with God, and the Word was God." (John 1:1) John the Baptist's role was "to testify to the light, so that all might believe through him." (v. 7). "The true light, which enlightens everyone, was coming into the world." (v. 9).

In these brief beginning passages of the gospels we are introduced to Jesus Christ as the Son of God and we are told that he is the Messiah; Jesus' human ancestry is traced and his divine nature revealed. These four different perspectives of the life of Jesus come together to form the gospel: the good news.

Jesus came to Galilee, proclaiming the good news of God and saying, 'The time is fulfilled, and the kingdom of God has come near; repent, and believe in the good news.'

Mark 1:14-15

Heavenly Father, we give thanks to you for the "good news" in the person of your Son, Jesus Christ, our Redeemer. Give us strength to repent our sins and faith to believe all that has been revealed to us. *Amen.*

Psalm 85:1-2, 8-13;
Isaiah 40:1-11; 2 Peter 3:8-15a; *Mark 1:1-8*

20

Monday   Week of Advent 2

A Stronghold in Times of Trouble

The Lord is a stronghold for the oppressed,
a stronghold in times of trouble.

Psalm 9:9

Who were the oppressed in Jesus' time? Israel was occupied by the Romans. The census that was said to have occurred at the time of Jesus' birth was a means of taxing the Jews; no apparent thought given to its inconvenience. Even the Jewish religious leaders answered to the Roman authorities. But were the Romans the only oppressors?

Appeasement of the Roman rulers was how the Jewish leaders walked a fine line between loss of control over their own people and loss of position and authority to the Romans. This is most pronounced in the gospels during the trial and condemnation of Jesus. The Jewish leaders were fearful that the growing popularity of Jesus would cause trouble with the Roman Empire, and they were jealous of that popularity. They plotted to use the words and actions of Jesus against him.

The Jewish leaders also knew they had limited control over how they could silence Jesus. They manipulated Pilate by pressing the Roman governor to prosecute Jesus and by stirring up the local population against him. Jesus was as much a victim of the oppression of the Jewish leaders as he was of the Roman authorities.

Today oppression continues all around the world in many forms. In some Arab countries the people have risen up against governments and leaders who impoverish their people and deprive them of basic freedoms. Cruel and vindictive dictators are even slaughtering their own people to hold on to power. In other countries warring tribal factions are preventing needed supplies from reaching starving people, and in some places the relief food is stolen and then sold back to the needy people at exorbitant prices.

Here in the United States oppression occurs at the community level. Foreign workers are coerced into living in inhuman conditions and accepting substandard wages. Children and women are forced to be sex slaves. Families become homeless because of the unscrupulousness of greedy financiers.

In Roman times, in other countries and in our states and cities, "The Lord is a stronghold for the oppressed, a stronghold in times of trouble." (Psalm 9:9). God is present with the victims of oppression whether that person is our Lord or a tiny child. God protects the innocent and the helpless. "For the needy shall not always be forgotten, nor the hope of the poor perish forever." (Psalm 9:18)

> *Look with pity, O heavenly Father, upon the people in this land who live with injustice, terror, disease, and death as their constant companions. Have mercy upon us. Help us to eliminate our cruelty to these our neighbors....*

"For the Oppressed," *The Book of Common Prayer*, 826

Merciful God, many of your people suffer. Have pity on them, save them from hatred and cruelty. Show us how we can be the servants of your love and compassion to those in need. *Amen.*

AM: Psalm 25; PM: *Psalm 9*, 15;
Amos 7:1-9; Revelation 1:1-8; Matthew 22:23-33

Tuesday   Week of Advent 2

The Shepherd's Staff

I am the good shepherd.

John 10:14

The candy cane is a common sight at Christmas, and a favorite of the children. Today it comes in many flavors and colors but traditionally it is red and white striped. There are various stories about the origin and meaning of the candy cane. One story says that the candy cane's shape represents a shepherd's staff, a metaphor often used in Christianity for Jesus, the Good Shepherd. It has even been said that the white represents the purity and love of Jesus and the red the blood he shed for us.

Shepherds and sheep have been identified with Christ from the time of his birth. Angels first announced the birth of Jesus to shepherds. "To you is born this day in the city of David a Saviour, who is the Messiah, the Lord." (Luke 2:11)

The prophet Amos was a shepherd who preached repentance to the people of Israel much as John the Baptist did. "And the Lord took me from following the flock, and the Lord said to me, 'Go, prophesy to my people Israel.'" (Amos 7:14) The words of Amos were harsh words of God's judgment against a people that had strayed away from the Lord's teachings. "Therefore I will punish you for all your iniquities." (Amos 3:2)

We, too, stray away from the righteous path of God and Jesus must come to call us home. Jesus knows of our wandering

23

ways. He is the Good Shepherd and he knows his sheep. "I am the good shepherd. I know my own and my own know me. (John 10:14)

When you hang candy canes on your Christmas tree this year, or pass them out to children, or enjoy one yourself, look at its shape, and remember the story. Think of our Good Shepherd, the one who hunts for the lost sheep and carries them home.

> *If a shepherd has a hundred sheep, and one of them has gone astray, does he not leave the ninety-nine on the mountains and go in search of the one that went astray? And if he finds it, truly I tell you, he rejoices over it more than over the ninety-nine that never went astray. So it is not the will of your Father in heaven that one of these little ones should be lost.*
>
> Matthew 18:12-14

Jesus, when we sin we are like sheep who stray from the foal. When we are lost from you search us out and carry us home. *Amen.*

AM: Psalm 26, 28; PM: Psalm 36, 39;
Amos 7:10-17; Revelation 1:9-16; Matthew 22:34-46

Wednesday   Week of Advent 2

The Words of the Lord

The time is surely coming, says the Lord God,
when I will send a famine on the land;
not a famine of bread, or a thirst for water,
but of hearing the words of the Lord.

Amos 8:11

Over and over in the Old Testament prophets warned the people of Israel that God would punish them for their wickedness. God threatened famines, pestilence and destitution. He predicted war and occupation. Nothing seemed to change the desire of the Israelites to continue their evil ways. Even when they repented and turned away from worshipping false idols, they soon returned to their sinful practices.

When the Israelites wandered in the desert and cried out for food and water the Lord heard their prayers and provided for them. Yet in this passage Amos tells us that their behavior had not changed. And God is so angry that he will visit upon his people a punishment much harsher than any physical denial. "I will send a famine on the land; not a famine of bread, or a thirst for water, but of hearing the words of the Lord." (Amos 8:11). The body will die without water and proper nourishment; the soul will perish without the word of God.

A famine grips the country of Somalia right now. And we whose bellies are always full cannot even begin to imagine the horror of it. We see pictures of emaciated children and dying babies. We hear mothers tell of leaving dead children along the trail because they are too weak to carry them and too weak to dig their graves.

25

Even in the face of this kind of famine, I would more greatly fear a famine "of hearing the words of the Lord." The words of the Lord have been a part of my life even before the time I could understand what they were. I first learned about the words of God in my catechism and read them in the Bible. I studied the words of the Lord intensely in seminary.

On Sundays I hear the word of God read in the lessons and preached about in the sermon. I seek comfort from God's words in time of trouble. I meditate on God's precious words. These meditations are based on God's word.

My whole being would feel as dry as the desert without the words of the Lord. My heart would faint for those words. My soul would thirst for them. I live for those words.

Oh, Lord, take not away your word from your people. Do not abandon us. We are a sinful people, just as the Israelites were, and we do deserve punishment.

If you take away your words, Lord, how will we know when we have erred and strayed? How will we know your will? How will we know the truth of your Word? And how will we hear the good news of Jesus Christ and his saving grace? How will we know you sent the Spirit to guide us?

Take not away your word, but use it to teach us, to lead us, to guide us and heal us. *Amen.*

AM: Psalm 38; PM: Psalm 119:25-48;
Amos 8:1-14; Revelation 1:17-2:7; Matthew 23:1-12

Thursday   Week of Advent 2

First Clean the Inside of the Cup

*First clean the inside of the cup
so that the outside also may become clean.*

Matthew 13:26

The Pharisees often sought to discredit Jesus for disregarding the rites and rituals of the Jews. How could he be a leader of the Jewish people when he did not even follow the basic rules? In this passage from Matthew, Jesus pointed out that all the time spent on extensive external cleansing rituals neglected the inner spiritual cleansing that was more important. "Woe to you, scribes and Pharisees, hypocrites! For you clean the outside of the cup and of the plate, but inside they are full of greed and self-indulgence. You blind Pharisee! First clean the inside of the cup, so that the outside also may become clean." (Matthew 23:25-26).

For the Pharisees outward appearances were important. If their rituals and religious practices showed them to be holy and pious, other people would judge them to be so. But Jesus knew better. "So you also on the outside look righteous to others, but inside you are full of hypocrisy and lawlessness." (v. 28).

It is the desire of our Lord that we focus first and foremost on the "inside of our cup." "Do not be conformed to this world, but be transformed by the renewing of your minds, so that you may discern what the will of God— what is good and acceptable and perfect." (Romans 12:2). Our inward reflection on righteousness is reflected outside ourselves by our actions. When we practice sound thinking and good judgment we make choices that are good for ourselves and for others. Exhibitions of piety or purity are not necessary. Our words and actions speak for themselves. We are doing the will of God.

The readings during Advent give us many opportunities to see how pride and arrogance corrupt, and to consider the consequences of sinful behavior. Lessons in the Old Testament from Amos, Isaiah and others tell of how the people of God turned away from him and how God responded. "All the sinners of my people shall die by the sword." (Amos 9:10). Jesus responded angrily to the same sort of behavior practiced by the Pharisees. "Thus you testify against yourselves that you are descendants of those who murdered the prophets." (Matthew 23:31)

In the Advent Epistle readings we also read words of warning about being led astray and losing focus on personal integrity. "You therefore, beloved, since you are forewarned, beware that you are not carried away with the error of the lawless and lose your own stability." (1 Peter 3:17.) And Jude offered his own words of advice. "But you, beloved, build yourselves up on your most holy faith; pray in the Holy Spirit; keep yourselves in the love of God; look forward to the mercy of our Lord Jesus Christ that leads to eternal life." (Jude 1:20)

God gave us minds so we could think and make decisions for ourselves. God also gave us prophets, leaders and teachers to help us discern his holy will for us. And the Son of God in the flesh was the perfect example of obedience to the will of God.

When our minds are focused on the word of the Lord we remain pure in spirit and we are free from sin. This is a continual process of inner renewal and outward action. When we are cleansed and purified inwardly we shine with the light of Christ and that light shines outwardly for all to see.

God, you gave us the gift of minds to think and free wills to act. May our minds always guide us in your righteous path, reflecting your love in all that we say and do. *Amen.*

AM: Psalm 37:1-18; PM: Psalm 37:19-42;
Amos 9:1-10; Revelation 2:8-17; **Matthew 23:13-26**

Friday   Week of Advent 2

My House Lies in Ruins

My house lies in ruins,
while all of you hurry off to your own houses.

Haggai 1:9

In the prophet Haggai's time God was desirous that the temple in Jerusalem be rebuilt. Yet the people declared they were not ready to do so. "These people say the time has not yet come to rebuild the Lord's house." (Haggai 1:2) He sees people putting more energy into their own personal dwellings rather than in rebuilding God's house of worship. "My house lies in ruins, while all of you hurry off to your own houses." (Haggai 1:9)

God invites the Jewish people to consider the consequences of their actions:

> *Now therefore, thus says the LORD of hosts: Consider how you have fared. You have sown much, and harvested little; you eat, but you never have enough; you drink, but you never have your fill; you clothe yourselves, but no one is warm; and you that earn wages earn wages to put them into a bag with holes.*
>
> Haggai 1:5-6

God had withheld water and good harvests from the people, "therefore the heavens above you have withheld the dew, and the earth has withheld its produce," (v. 10) to remind them he provided the means for their bodies to be filled. Even when the people focused on providing food, clothing and funds for themselves, they were not satisfied. Satisfaction comes from

29

being filled and from fulfillment. Haggai's massage from God is that the people will not feel a sense of satisfaction until they are fulfilled as well as filled and that fulfillment does not come from food and drink but from obeying the word of God.

Eating and drinking and the means for survival are necessary but they do not fill a person in the way that prayer and worship does. When the temple is rebuilt the people will have an appropriate place to worship God. They will feel satisfaction in their accomplishment and the Lord will provide for them.

We eat, we drink, but do we always feel satisfied? How many times do you find yourselves looking through your cabinets or combing through your refrigerator just a short time after you have eaten? What is lacking in your diet that you do not feel filled?

Your bank balance looks good, you have money in your pocket, but you don't feel like you are satisfied. Are you putting your wages "into a bag with holes"? Is your life as empty as that money bag?

The book of Haggai written by the prophet in 520 B.C.E is a challenge by God for people to stop thinking only of themselves and to begin working together to rebuild the temple in Jerusalem. The temple was a work of brick and stone. But another kind of temple needed to be rebuilt. That was the temple in the heart of the Jewish people. What kind of a temple do we need to rebuild?

This message from God is not about the lack of basic needs but the emptiness that we feel when we are seeking out the wrong things to keep us satisfied. God can fill our emptiness. We have only to let our lives be a temple for him.

Heavenly Father, you provide all things necessary for our existence. Help us to appreciate your gifts and to understand all that we need to filled and fulfilled. *Amen.*

AM: Psalm 31; PM: Psalm 35;
Haggai 1:1-15; Revelation 2:18-29; Matthew 23:27-39

Saturday   Week of Advent 2

The Perfectionist in me and my God

I have not found your works
perfect in the sight of my God.

Revelation 3:2

"I have not found your works perfect." (Revelations 3:2) Wow! And I thought I was a perfectionist (at least in some things). God wants us to be perfect. He certainly wants a lot from us lowly humans. (Of course he did make us in *his* image.)

God wants our works to be without flaw or defect. That's one meaning of perfect, and it is a tough one. As I pondered this I thought of an example from my Christmas preparations that could fit this definition of perfect, but this example also brought to mind another definition that might be more fitting.

One of my favorite parts about Christmas is decorating my Christmas tree. I have many beautiful ornaments. Some I made; others were made for me. Some were gifts from friends or family. As I carefully choose a spot for each of these special ornaments I recall the family member or friend and the special memories connected with the piece.

When I decorate my Christmas tree I first place the star on top and then very carefully arrange every light on the tree, switching bulbs around if necessary to make sure that the colors are balanced. Next I drape the garland, adjusting it so it drapes gracefully on the limbs of the tree. Then I find a place to hang a black boot that has a long tube that extends down the tree into the water basin. This is a neat little gadget that enables me to water the tree without disturbing the skirt and gifts.

When all of this is complete I can finally begin to add

the decorations. Most of my decorations are still kept in their original boxes and I begin to take them out one by one. I have some favorites I like to place on first. One is a raccoon hanging from a candy cane. Others are nativity scenes, birds and angels. I have three different size icicles that I place near the ends of the large branches.

And then I have a dozen or more each of snowflakes, stars and bells that are translucent and glow in the dark. I try to make sure I spread then evenly about the tree so I can turn off all the lights at night and see them glowing in the dark. If my tree is large enough with a lot of small branches I also add a whole collection of small wooden ornaments that came from a special Advent wreath one of my sisters gave me. The very last decoration is a beautiful ceramic nativity scene placed on blue velvet under the tree. When I used to put tinsel on my tree I hung it one strand at a time. It would take me days to do that! I really want my tree to be perfect.

Yes, you are saying, that is the work of a perfectionist. I agree. I want it to be perfect. But I also want something else. I want to feel it is complete. I think that is what God wants of us. Another definition of perfect is to be complete. When we fulfill God's perfect plan for us, then we are complete.

At Christmas we celebrate the coming of Jesus into the world. Jesus is the perfect offering for our sins. He is the completion of God's perfect plan for our salvation.

Heavenly Father, accept the offering of my Christmas tree as a gift I give in celebration of the birth of your only Son, my Lord and my Redeemer. Neither this gift nor my life are without flaw or defect; please help me to fulfill your perfect plan for me. *Amen.*

AM: Psalm 30, 32; PM: Psalm 42, 43;
Haggai 2:1-9; *Revelation 3:1-6*; Matthew 24:1-14

Advent 3

Your promise gives me life.

Psalm 119:50

Sunday   Third Sunday of Advent

Rejoice!

I will greatly rejoice in the LORD,
my whole being shall exult in my God.

Isaiah 61:10

The readings for the third Sunday of Advent are a reprieve from the dire warnings of the prophets and from the wrath of God that has rained down the past two weeks. These readings help us focus forward on the birth of our Savior. It is time to get excited about the impending commemoration of Jesus' birth.

On this Sunday we anticipate with much joy the coming of our Redeemer. Many phrases sing out with love for God and his gift of salvation; many voices bring us the good news. Let us rejoice at the coming of Jesus and his coming again!

At the announcement of the incarnation Mary's spirit breaks forth in praise of God. "My soul magnifies the Lord, and my spirit rejoices in God my Saviour." (Luke 1:46-47) In Isaiah the prophet uses similar words in proclaiming salvation:

> *I will greatly rejoice in the LORD,*
> *my whole being shall exult in my God;*
> *for he has clothed me with the garments of salvation,*
> *he has covered me with the robe of righteousness.*

Isaiah 61:10

Mary echoes the joy of the fulfillment of God's promise to

35

Israel:

> *He has helped his servant Israel,*
> *in remembrance of his mercy,*
> *according to the promise he made to our ancestors,*
> *to Abraham and to his descendants for ever.*

Luke 1:54-55

These voices rejoice not only in the news they bring but in the anointing of the Spirit that allows them to be prophets of the Word.

> *The spirit of the Lord God is upon me,*
> *because the Lord has anointed me;*
> *he has sent me to bring good news to the*
> *oppressed,*
> *to bind up the broken-hearted,*
> *to proclaim liberty to the captives,*
> *and release to the prisoners;*
> *to proclaim the year of the LORD's favour.*

Isaiah 61:1

We, too, should rejoice that we are anointed to bring the good news of Jesus Christ! Advent and Christmas give us great opportunities to share our faith in Jesus Christ. A faithful life in Christ will also lead to rejoicing when Jesus comes again. "May the God of peace himself sanctify you entirely; and may your spirit and soul and body be kept sound and blameless at the coming of our Lord Jesus Christ." (1 Thessalonians 5:23)

Jesus, our Lord and Savior, we rejoice at the celebration of your birth and we seek a life worthy of rejoicing when you shall come to claim us again. *Amen.*

Psalm 126 or *Canticle* 3 or *15*; *Isaiah 61:1-4, 8-11; 1 Thessalonians 5:16-24*; John 1:6-8,19-28

Monday   Week of Advent 3

Listen to what the Spirit is saying to the Churches

Let anyone who has an ear
listen to what the Spirit is saying to the churches.

Revelation 3:13

The first part of this verse is found in various forms in the synoptic gospels as well as in the Book of Revelation. "And he said, 'Let anyone with ears to hear listen!'" (Mark 4:9) It acts as a kind refrain in John's letter to the seven churches. As a saying familiarly associated with Jesus it becomes an appropriate exhortation from the risen Christ.

It is the second half of the verse that caught my attention though. "Listen to what the spirit is saying to the churches." The Spirit obviously had a lot to say to the churches in the Book of Revelation. My question is, "What is the Spirit saying to the churches now?"

Sitting in a half empty church this question seems appropriate enough. In a sermon recently we were told that during a decade of evangelism in the Episcopal Church membership actually decreased. What does that mean? Did evangelism in the Episcopal Church fail? Did members leave the Episcopal Church to go to Evangelical churches? We were not given an explanation.

Church attendance is declining in many denominations. Surveys are done; articles written. Some explanations are offered. Young adults today do not follow the patterns of their parents in attending church, the music is not contemporary enough, etc.

In the Episcopal Church declining attendance has been blamed on the ordination of women, the ordination of openly gay bishops and more generally a departure from the traditional teachings of the church. Some of these issues have caused a severe strain in relations with the Anglican Communion. This has led to the desire to develop a more formal covenant relationship. Will that make a difference? What does? What will?

Something gets people to church sometimes. Think about Easter and Christmas. There are always more people in church then. Why? An answer might be because these are important days in the church year. People want to be there. So something does get people to church sometimes. Are not Sundays important days in the life of the church? Is the work of the church not important enough? Do we make visible and apparent to the outside world what is most important to us, important enough for people to want to be a part of it?

Other question to ponder are: "What is, or is not happening in the churches that keeps people away?" What is the spirit in the churches? Is the Spirit present in the churches?

What is the Spirit saying to the churches? I do not know. What I do know is that the churches had better listen.

Spirit, we are your people. Breathe your life into us that we may find a way to breathe life into your churches. Guide us in ways that we can carry the Word into the world, and in turn invite the world into our churches. *Amen.*

AM: Psalm 41, 52; PM: Psalm 44;
Zechariah 1:7-17; **Revelation 3:7-13**; Matthew 24:15-31

Tuesday   Week of Advent 3

No One Knows

But about that day and hour no one knows, neither the angels of heaven, nor the Son, but only the Father.

Matthew 24:36

I just shake my head at the words and images that come to mind when I read this passage. I am remembering a news story about a man who declared that he knew the exact day and hour of the end of the world. He received quite a bit of publicity. He was even the fodder of late night comedians. He and his followers made preparations. One man paid for a large roadside sign advertising the world's end. Some people gave away their possessions or wealth.

I also remember that this was not the first time this man had made such a prediction. When the end did not come as originally predicted, the man said he must have miscalculated. And then there he was again, predicting the end, very self-righteous, very self confident.

The day and time came —and went and life on earth went on. And there were more jokes.

I saw a picture of this man on the Internet. He looked old, tired and bewildered. I felt sorry for him. It had to have been very embarrassing to have God show you up in such a big way. At the same time I felt sorry for this man's followers, especially those who had given away what they had because they believed his prediction.

It is quite natural to want to know when the end of the world is coming. Advance warning does give you a chance to be prepared. However, in the Gospel of Matthew Jesus is quite clear who knows, and who doesn't know. "Keep awake therefore, for *you* [emphasis added] do not know on what day your Lord is coming." (Matthew 24:42)

Jesus' disciples wanted to know when the end was coming, too. So they went to him "privately" and asked him, "Tell us, when will this be, and what will be the sign of your coming and of the end of the age?" (v.3). Jesus answered their question with a long discourse on false prophets, disasters, and persecutions. As to the appointed time Jesus replied, "But about that day and hour no one knows, neither the angels of heaven, nor the Son, but only the Father." (v.36) Did the man who kept declaring he knew when the world would end miss this chapter of Matthew?

Certain signs or events may or may not point to the end of the world. No one on earth knows that for sure. Jesus warns us always to be prepared. "Therefore you also must be ready, for the Son of Man is coming at an unexpected hour." (v.42)

Even as I see in my mind this man's picture, I also can envision our heavenly Father, sitting on the throne of heaven with a rather amused, but caring look on his face. And he is probably shaking his head, too. And maybe he is thinking, "Didn't he hear what my Son said: "only the Father."

Heavenly Father, sometimes it seems we want to know too much. Rather than put our trust in you we want things to happen our way by our timetables. We forget that you are the master of the universe and all time is in your hands. Help us to surrender our lives to you so that we can be prepared when the Son of man returns again —whenever that may be. *Amen.*

AM: Psalm 45; PM: Psalm 47, 48;
Zechariah 2:1-13; Revelation 3:14-22; *Matthew 24:32-44*

Wednesday   Week of Advent 3

Your Promise gives me Life

Remember your word to your servant,
in which you have made me hope.
This is my comfort in my distress,
that your promise gives me life.

Psalm 119:49-50

Before the birth of Jesus the Israelites held on to their hope in the promise of God that they would be restored as children of God and heirs of his eternal kingdom. In Psalm 119 the psalmist reminds us that hope from God is very comforting; it sustains us in our time of need. The words of this psalm also remind us that we need to make a commitment to God. God expects us to keep his commandments just as he kept his promise:

The Lord is my portion;
I promise to keep your words.
I implore your favour with all my heart;
be gracious to me according to your promise.

Psalm 119:57-58

More than a dozen times in the Old Testament our heavenly Father reminds us to be faithful to his commandments. "Thus says the Lord of hosts: If you will walk in my ways and keep my requirements." (Zechariah 3:7) And Jesus echoes his Father's words in the Gospel of John. "If you keep my commandments, you will abide in my love, just as I have kept my Father's commandments and abide in his love." (John 15.10)

You have dealt well with your servant,
O Lord, according to your word.
Teach me good judgement and knowledge,
for I believe in your commandments.

Psalm 119:65-66

As a servant obeys his master, we are called to obey the word of God. In John's Gospel Jesus says, "Blessed is that slave whom his master will find at work when he arrives." (John 24:46). If we keep the commandments of God we will receive our reward just as this slave is rewarded.

What is our reward? Jesus Christ has fulfilled the promise of redemption. And through his saving grace we are rewarded with eternal life.

Let your heart hold fast my words;
keep my commandments, and live.

Proverbs 4:4

Dear Jesus, We strive to keep your Father's commandments. It is our hope that when we stand before you on our judgment day that you will say: "Well done good and faithful servant." *Amen.*

AM: Psalm 119:49-72; PM: Psalm 49, [53];
Zechariah 3:1-10; Revelation 4:1-8*; Matthew 24:45-51*

Thursday   Week of Advent 3

Do I eat the flesh of bulls,
or drink the blood of goats?

If I were hungry, I would not tell you,
for the world and all that is in it is mine.
Do I eat the flesh of bulls, or drink the blood of goats?

Psalm 50:12-13

The title given to this Psalm is, "The Acceptable Sacrifice." One can almost hear the derision in the voice of God: "Do I eat the flesh of bulls, or drink the blood of goats?" Clearly these were not God's idea of acceptable sacrifices. All things are created by God. He could have his pick. "If I were hungry, I would not tell you, for the world and all that is in it is mine." We acknowledge that all belongs to God when we use these words from 1 Chronicles as our offerings are presented in our worship service: "For all things come from you, and of your own have we given you." (1 Chronicles 29:14).

God is not refusing sacrifice by the people. "Not for your sacrifices do I rebuke you; Your burnt-offerings are continually before me." (Psalm 50:8) Rather, the people seemed to misunderstand the reason for sacrifices to God. Sacrifice to God is in thanksgiving for his many blessings. "Offer to God a sacrifice of thanksgiving, and pay your vows to the Most High" (Psalm 50:14) In this day's reading from the Book of Revelation a prayer (or song) can be found that would be most acceptable to God:

You are worthy, our Lord and God,
to receive glory and honour and power,
for you created all things,

43

and by your will they existed and were created.

Revelation 4:11

People offer what they consider most valuable or important to them. Animals were important possessions in biblical times so it does make some sense that people in ancient Israel would offer them as sacrifices. We know that people also gave financial donations in those times to support the temple just as today we give financial offerings to support the church.

The problem may be that we see these materialistic offerings as all we can or need to give to God. Whether in ancient times or today we can get so caught up in materialistic things that we do not think about thanking God, offering praise or worshipping God. Setting aside time regularly to attend worship services, singing hymns of praise, or offering humble words of thanksgiving for the blessings we have received are just a few ways we can make acceptable sacrifices to God. This Advent and Christmas season are very appropriate times to develop good habits of prayer, praise and thanksgiving.

Those who bring thanksgiving as their sacrifice honour me;
to those who go the right way
I will show the salvation of God.

Psalm 50:23

Gracious and loving Father, you are most worthy of all our praise and worship. Thank you for all the many blessings of our lives. We give thanks to you for the gift of Jesus Christ you Son and our Redeemer, and the Holy Spirit, our guide and our comforter. Glory and praise be to thee for ever and ever. *Amen.*

AM: *Psalm 50*; PM: Psalm [59, 60] or 33;
Zechariah 4:1-14; *Revelation 4:9-5:5;* Matthew 25:1-13

44

Friday   Week of Advent 3

The Wrath of God?

Render true judgements,
show kindness and mercy.

Zechariah 7:8

This is another one of those passages from the Old Testament about God's wrath that I struggle to believe. I wonder how many of the reports of terrible things caused by God's wrath were not at least filtered though a layer of guilt or perhaps they were an attempt to explain the unexplainable. When bad things happen to the people of God there must be an explanation. Maybe we deserved it, but God did it. Divine intervention of the worse kind.

Word came from God saying, "Render true judgements, show kindness and mercy to one another; do not oppress the widow, the orphan, the alien, or the poor; and do not devise evil in your hearts against one another." (Zechariah 7:9-10.) Still the people disobeyed God. "They refused to listen, and turned a stubborn shoulder, and stopped their ears in order not to hear," (v.11) and so God's wrath was visited upon them. "I scattered them with a whirlwind among all the nations that they had not known. Thus the land they left was desolate." (v.14) What happened to the kindness and mercy?

Then God has second thoughts. "Thus says the Lord of hosts: I will save my people from the east country and from the west country; and I·will bring them to live in Jerusalem." Is this God feeling guilty? Well, if God can feel wrathful, why not guilty? And these sound more like the words of a merciful God: "They shall be my people and I will be their God, in faithfulness and in righteousness." (Zechariah 8:8)

45

In today's world we have different kinds of "prophets" delivering messages they make think are divinely inspired. They feel justified in declaring earthquakes and hurricanes are the result of the behavior of certain "sinful" people. At the same time we have people skeptical of explanations for certain weather phenomena that include the possibility of climate change. Is God responsible for all of this as well?

The answer is yes, and no. I believe that God is the Creator of all things but I do not believe that God manipulates nature for purposes of punishment. When I listen to news of tornados or floods wiping out large parts of town, I do not think, "Well, God has taken care of those sinful people!" In the Bible we can find numerous examples of when God was merciful. In very community affected by natural disasters and adverse weather all over the world there are sinners of all stripes, for none of us are sinless, but I don't think God is picking on some places to use as an example to the rest of us.

Most people today seek out answers to weather phenomena through science. Individuals can choose or not to believe the scientific evidence. In biblical times, without such information to rely on, it would have been understandable that people looked to themselves and to God to provide answers. Is it so different today?

So do I blame today's sweltering heat or last winter's blizzard on God, on Mother Nature or on La Nina? Some people blame the weatherman. Me, I'll keep praying for "seasonable" weather for us all.

God of mercy, we thank you for all of your creation. Protect us from the dangers and disasters of this world. Grant to us all seasonable weather and an abundance of the fruits of the earth. *Amen.*

AM: Psalm 40, 54; PM: Psalm 51;
Zechariah 7:8-8:8; Revelation 5:6-14; Matthew 25:14-30

Saturday   Week of Advent 3

Let There Be Peace on Earth

For there shall be a sowing of peace.

Zechariah 8:12

Do you ever wonder what it would take for there to be peace on earth? Can you imagine a world with no wars? What would it be like to live in a world where all nations, races and individuals were living together in harmony?

True peace is surely something we long for, we greatly desire, but if seems elusive if not impossible. Many pieces of literature deal with the subject of peace. One of the most well known of these is a Christmas carol, "I Heard the Bells on Christmas Day." The words are from a poem, "Christmas Bells," by Henry Wadsworth Longfellow:

And in despair I bowed my head;
"There is no peace on earth," I said;
"For hate is strong,
And mocks the song
Of peace on earth, good-will to men!"

Then pealed the bells more loud and deep:
"God is not dead; nor doth he sleep!
The Wrong shall fail,
The Right prevail,
With peace on earth, good-will to men!"

"Christmas Bells," Henry Wadsworth Longfellow, 1864

47

During the Christmas season I think we long for that peace even more. I have heard stories of armies laying down their arms and singing Christmas carols together across enemy lines on Christmas Eve. If only we could live that kind of peace every day.

One of the titles given to Jesus by Isaiah at his birth is "Prince of Peace." Isaiah goes on to say, "His authority shall grow continually, and there shall be endless peace." (Isaiah 9:7). Did that mean Jesus' mission was to bring about peace on the earth? In the gospels of Matthew and Luke, Jesus states that it is not so. "Do not think that I have come to bring peace to the earth; I have not come to bring peace, but a sword." (Matthew 10:34) "Do you think that I have come to bring peace to the earth? No, I tell you, but rather division!" (Luke 12:51) In both of these passages Jesus says that family members will be turned against one another. That does not sound like peace to me!

In Matthew's gospel Jesus goes on to talk of taking up our cross and following him. With Jesus and in Jesus is where we will find our peace. Jesus did not come into the world to "impose" peace, but to "sow peace": to teach us how to find God's peace in ourselves and to share that peace in our hearts with others. We practice that sharing of God's peace with the "passing of the peace" during our worships services on Sundays.

No matter clichéd it sounds, peace starts with the individual. I must somehow find a way to say to Satan, "Get behind me," when I struggle with thoughts of anger and jealousy. I must learn to forgive those who wrong me and seek to make peace with those I have wronged.

Blessed Jesus, Prince of Peace, Let there be peace on earth, and let it begin with me. *Amen.*

AM: Psalm 55; PM: Psalm 138, 139:1-17(18-23); ***Zechariah 8:9-17***; Revelation 6:1-17; Matthew 25:31-46

Advent 4

What was promised through faith in Jesus Christ might be given to those who believe.

Galatians 3:22

Sunday   Fourth Sunday of Advent

Here Am I

Here am I, the servant of the Lord;
let it be with me according to your word.

Luke 1:38

Mary! Sometimes all I can do is marvel at her reactions. One day the Angel Gabriel dropped by and said to her, "Greetings, favoured one! The Lord is with you." (Luke 1: 28). Mary was, like the rest of us might have been (to put it mildly), "much perplexed by his words and pondered what sort of greeting this might be." (v. 29) I do believe I would have been more than "perplexed." If an angel of the Lord suddenly appeared to me I might be surprised, astonished, or excited. Actually Gabriel's greeting might have given me some comfort; being called a "favoured one" and hearing "The Lord is with you," might at least have led me to believe I was not in some kind of big trouble.

Gabriel told Mary not to be afraid "for you have found favour with God." (v.30) (Big relief there.), and then gave her the big news: "you will conceive in your womb and bear a son, and you will name him Jesus. He will be great, and will be called the Son of the Most High, and the Lord God." (v.31). After this jaw-dropping, astounding, beyond-belief news, Mary, always the intelligent and practical one responded: "How can this be, since I am a virgin?" (v.34) Gabriel gave a complex answer to that question first. "The Holy Spirit will come upon you, and the power of the Most High will overshadow you; therefore the child to be born will be holy; he will be called Son of God." (v.35) The simple answer followed after Gabriel told Mary that her cousin Elizabeth (who was past her child-bearing years) was also going to have a baby, "For nothing will be impossible with God." (v.37).

That's all Mary needed to hear. And her response said it all. She was an obedient servant of her Lord. What an amazing (and very young) woman! Too often Mary is portrayed as much older than she probably would have been. I read a book last year that characterized Mary as really still almost a child who would rather stay at home with her mother than go off and live with a much older man. Even in what I considered to be a more realistic portrayal, Mary proceeded gamely with God's plan that the Angel Gabriel presented to her.

I never grow tired of hearing Mary's story; it always stirs my soul. Now deep in December we are nearing the culmination of the Advent season, and this passage from Luke begins the telling of the Christmas story. Soon we will reach that glorious night when Mary gave birth to that holy child she had carried for nine months. What a moment that must been for her!

In the gospel of Matthew we are told that after Jesus' birth wise men from the east came with gifts. And Joseph was warned in a dream not to go back to his home so they went to Egypt. Even these brief images of Mary's role in the life of Jesus are truly remarkable. All of this came about because of her quiet, calm words: "Here am I, the servant of the Lord; let it be with me according to your word." (Luke 1:38) If only we could respond with such simplicity to God's calls to us. We usually have some conditions and exceptions. The response we give usually sounds more like a "maybe." Our response should be an even more emphatic, "Yes, Lord, oh yes indeed! Here I am."

Gracious Lord, May we always be as ready as Mary was to respond to your word. *Amen.*

Canticle 3 or 15 or Psalm 89:1-4, 19-26;
2 Samuel 7:1-11, 16; Romans 16:25-27; *Luke 1:26-38*

Monday   Week of Advent 4

God Alone

For God alone my soul waits in silence.

Psalm 62:1

"For God alone my soul waits in silence." Psalm 62 begins with this beautiful line. "For God alone." Who else, above all would we wait for? God is all to us. He is our Creator, our Redeemer, and our Comforter. God is the ultimate: "He alone is my rock and my salvation." (v.2). Why God? "On God rests my deliverance and my honour; my mighty rock, my refuge is in God." (v.7) We have received our very life and nature from God. We are created in his image. Who else then could possibly be our greatest source of strength and refuge?

"My soul waits." Sometimes it seems there is nothing else we can do. All we can do is wait. We can't change anything. We have only yesterday, and we must wait on God for tomorrow. It is then that we need to be still. We need to wait in that quiet and lonely space between what was and will be, but is not quite now. We can appreciate such a space only in silence.

Elijah was told to go out and wait for the Lord.

He said, 'Go out and stand on the mountain before the Lord, for the Lord is about to pass by.' Now there was a great wind, so strong that it was splitting mountains and breaking rocks in pieces before the Lord, but the Lord was not in the wind; and after the wind an earthquake, but the

*Lord was not in the earthquake; and after the earthquake
a fire, but the Lord was not in the fire; and after the fire a
sound of sheer silence.*

1Kings 19:11-12

"Sheer silence." Pristine, pure and holy; it is in this silence
that you, like Elijah, will find God. God speaks into our silence.
God breathes life and meaning into our silence. God give us
strength and courage for facing what will be our tomorrows.
There in the silences comes the answer to our prayers. The
answer comes from God.

"For God alone my soul waits in silence, for my hope is
from him." (Psalm 62:5) Where else can we go to experience
such closeness, such intimacy with God? "Trust in him at all
times, O people; pour out your heart before him." (v.8) Alone in
the silence with God I can give all of myself, all of my sorrows
and joys to my Lord. And I can rejoice in his presence.

So what must we do? We must wait for God. Wait. Wait
alone. Wait in the silence. Wait for God. God will come. That is
what faith is about: believing that God will come. The chosen
people of God waited in that silence for God to come. They
waited a long time. They had faith. And God did come.

All the souls of all the people of the world waited for God
in the silence that is the emptiness without God. And then "the
Word became flesh." (John 1:14). Out of the silence prayers were
answered, promises were kept and souls were redeemed.

Thank you, *God,* for coming to us and for us where we wait
for you in the silence in our souls. *Amen.*

AM: ***Psalm*** 61, ***62***; PM: Psalm 112, 115;
Zephaniah 3:14-20; Titus 1:1-16; Luke 1:1-25

Tuesday   Week of Advent 4

Filled with the Spirit

The Holy Spirit will come upon you, and the power of the
Most High will overshadow you.

Luke 1:35

The first chapter of Luke's gospel mentions the Holy Spirit several times. The Angel Gabriel explained to Mary that she would conceive by the power of the Holy Spirit working in her. "The Holy Spirit will come upon you." (Luke 1:35) When Mary, pregnant with Jesus, visited Elizabeth, "the child leapt in her womb. And Elizabeth was filled with the Holy Spirit." (v.41). When John the Baptist was born, "his father Zechariah was filled with the Holy Spirit." (v.67) All of these three persons felt the Holy Spirit working in their lives in different ways. Mary would become the mother of the Savior through the direct intervention of the Holy Spirit in her life. Elizabeth is led by the Spirit to proclaim Mary and "the fruit of her womb" to be blessed. Zechariah is moved by the Holy Spirit to prophesy in thanksgiving and praise that God's people have received a savior in fulfillment of the Lord's word.

The Holy Spirit lives and dwells in us. Just as at the expected coming of Jesus people were moved by the Holy Spirit, so we, too, can be moved during the season of Advent. In fact, the Christmas season seems to be a time when we need to tap into the Spirit in us. Filled with God's Spirit we can be a blessing to others.

This time of year can be so hectic. Too much to do; not

enough time to do it. No parking spaces. Late to pick up the kids. What do we buy your father for Christmas? When will we get these presents wrapped or the tree decorated? Oh my gosh the cookies are burning! We lose patience with others and with ourselves. We forget to take time, let the Spirit fill us, and feel the Spirit in us.

So take a deep breath. It is time to take a deep breath —and breathe in the Holy Spirit. Let the Spirit slow you down, guide your thoughts, rest *your* weary spirit. Breathe it, feel it —the Holy Spirit within you. Let it be the Spirit of the season.

Stop, listen. Do you hear it? The Holy Spirit is in us and all around us: the Spirit of Christmas. The air is filled with the sound of beautiful Christmas carols, children laughing, bells ringing.

Look, do you see it? The Holy Spirit is coming forth from us. That man helping the lady with her packages. A corner kettle is overflowing with cash. Children's Christmas wishes being fulfilled via an Angel Tree.

Do you feel it? The Holy Spirit is in you; your spirit is resting in the Spirit of the Lord. Your pulse has slowed, your heart is beating slower, you are smiling. The Holy Spirit is working in your life and the lives of others.

A long time ago the Holy Spirit came upon Mary and Jesus was conceived. She said, "Let it be done to me according to your word." (38) We only have to open our hearts and the Spirit will enter into us as well.

Holy and life-giving Spirit, dwell in us and fill us with your grace and blessings. *Amen.*

AM: Psalm 66, 67; PM: Psalm 116, 117;
1 Samuel 2:1b-10; Titus 2:1-10; *Luke 1:26-38*

Wednesday   Week of Advent 4

According to Your Will

My soul magnifies the Lord,
and my spirit rejoices in God my Saviour,
for he has looked with favour
on the lowliness of his servant.

Luke 1:46-48

Reflecting on the title of Rick Warren's recent popular book, *The Purpose Driven Life,* I believe that I would prefer to have a purposeful life rather than a purpose-driven life. When I feel driven I often suffer anxiety that can make it hard to focus on my goals. I believe a purposeful life can have the same intensity of focus and direction without so much anxiety. If I am constantly working to fulfill my goals, to do the work God has called me to do, my life will be full of purpose.

The life of Mary, the mother of God, is one we can use as an example of a purposeful life. Mary's life took on a distinct focus and purpose after the angel Gabriel appeared to her and told her she would bear the son of God. She was to become the mother of the savior. She would be responsible for his care and upbringing as a child on earth. As I noted before, Mary responded to this astounding news with a calmness I regard with awe. "Here I am the servant of the Lord; let it be with according to your word." (Luke 1:38) This was not just any child; this was the Son of God. This was an awesome responsibility.

According to the Gospel of Luke, Mary did show a typical motherly anxiety when the boy Jesus was left behind in Jerusalem. "Child, why have you treated us like this? Look your father and

I have been searching for you with great anxiety." (Luke 2:48) However, she displayed a mother's confidence in her son at the wedding in Cana. "His mother said to the servants 'Do whatever he tells you.'" (John 2:5) She remained steadfast at her son's side through his torture and death. And after Jesus' death Mary continued to work with others to spread her son's message of love and salvation

Mary's life had great meaning and direction, dedicated to following the will of God. She rejoiced in the role God chose for her, and accepted it with humility.

And Mary said,
'My soul magnifies the Lord,
and my spirit rejoices in God my Saviour,
for he has looked with favour on the lowliness of his
servant.'

Luke 1:46-48

If we lead lives that have focus, dedication and direction we can achieve a purposeful life like that of Mary, the mother of God. We can have such purposeful lives by following her example. She accepted the will of God for her life, dedicated her life to the fulfillment of that role, and handled with grace and patience the many trials she endured.

Jesus, May I always look to your mother Mary as the perfect example of a purposeful life. May I always say with her, "Here I am. Let it be with me according to your will." *Amen.*

AM: Psalm 72; PM: Psalm 111, 113;
2 Samuel 7:1-17; Titus 2:11-3:8a; *Luke 1:39-48a (48b-56)*

Thursday   Week of Advent 4

Praise to the Lord

Praise the Lord!
Praise the Lord, O my soul!
I will praise the Lord as long as I live;
*   I will sing praises to my God all my life long.*

Psalm 146:1-2

"Praise the Lord, O my soul I will praise the Lord as long as I live." We do not have enough minutes, hours, days, weeks, months, or even years to praise God for all that he has done for us. That is why words of praise to God must always be in our hearts, on our minds; let us offer our praise in silent prayer, in joyous exclamation and in songs of praise. Let us give praise and worship to God at all times and in all ways!

We have so much to be thankful for. "He covers the heavens with clouds, / prepares rain for the earth, / makes grass grow on the hills. (Psalm 147:8-9) We breathe in fresh fall breezes after long, hot summers. The bright blue sky is endless; it is as endless as God's love and mercy.

God is good to his people.

The Lord lifts up those who are bowed down;
*   the Lord loves the righteous.*
The Lord watches over the strangers;
*   he upholds the orphan and the widow.*

Psalm 146:8-9

We have family and friends, we have sources of help and

inspiration, but ultimately it is only God on whom we can rely to provide all our needs. "Do not put your trust in princes, in mortals.... When their breath departs, they return to the earth." (Psalm 146:3-4)

Let us give thanks and praise to our God who knows and cares for each and every one of us. He knows our sorrows and our troubles. "He heals the broken-hearted, / and binds up their wounds." (Psalm 147:3).

Let us "sing to the LORD with thanksgiving." (v.7)

Praise to the Lord, O let all that is in me adore him!
All that hath life and breath, come now with praises before him.
Let the amen
sound from his people again,
gladly for ever adore him.

"Praise to the Lord," Joachim Neander, pub. 1680
English Translation, Catherine Winkworth, 1863

We owe to God all that we are and all that we have. Our praise and worship is but a small token of the thanks we feel within our hearts for all God's gifts and grace. Let us take time, as we draw near to the celebration of the birth of Jesus, to thank God for all his blessings.

Good and gracious God, We thank you for our lives and for your love. We praise you for all the goodness you work in our lives and for our many blessings. Most of all we thank you for Jesus Christ, our Lord and our Redeemer. *Amen.*

AM: Psalm 80; PM: ***Psalm 146, 147;***
2 Samuel 8:18-29; Galatians 3:1-14; Luke 1:57-66

Friday   Week of Advent 4

Those Who Believe

What was promised through faith in Jesus Christ
might be given to those who believe.

Galatians 3:22

The fulfillment of God's promise to Abraham to send a redeemer did not come from fulfillment of the law but from fulfillment of the promises made. "The law, which came four hundred and thirty years later, does not annul a covenant previously ratified by God, so as to nullify the promise. For if the inheritance comes from the law, it no longer comes from the promise; but God granted it to Abraham through the promise." (17-19) The law given to Moses was not meant to annul, invalidate, or deny the promises given to Abraham.

"Why then the law? It was added because of transgressions, until the offspring would come to whom the promise had been made; and it was ordained through angels by a mediator." (Galatians 3:19) God gave the law to Moses because of the sins of the Israelites. The people needed strict guidelines to follow; they were not acting out of faith but in obedience to the commandments of God. This law would be their rule of life until the "offspring," Jesus Christ would come.

The commandments were given to a mediator, Moses, and not brought by God himself. Jesus Christ brought the two "great" Commandments that would sum up all of the law. The first commandment: "You shall love the Lord your God with all your heart, and with all your soul, and with all your mind." And the second: 'You shall love your neighbour as yourself.' "On these two commandments hang all the law and the prophets." (Matthew 22:37-40)

Are the commandments given to Moses then in opposition to the teaching of Jesus? No, Jesus himself said: 'Do not think that I have come to abolish the law or the prophets; I have come not to abolish but to fulfil." (Matthew 5:17) The two commandments pronounced by Jesus were not meant to replace the law of Moses but rather offered a summation of what God required: love of God and love of others. God's love was the foundation of the law and the fulfillment of the promises made to Abraham.

The law of God showed all to be sinners. The effects of sin could not be nullified by obedience to the law alone; an acceptable sacrifice needed to be given for redemption. That sacrifice was made possible by the coming of Jesus, the Son of God, into the world. Jesus, the redeemer, was the fulfillment of the promises to Abraham.

By Jesus' sacrifice of himself the sins of the whole world were forgiven; the promise of redemption was fulfilled. "What was promised through faith in Jesus Christ might be given to those who believe." (Galatians 3:22) Those who believed in Jesus Christ were rewarded for their faith. Their sins were forgiven and they were given the promise of eternal life. The promises made to Abraham were thus fulfilled.

By our faith in Jesus Christ the promises made to Abraham are fulfilled in us. Our sins are forgiven. What is required of us is that we show our love of Christ through our love of God and one another.

Lord God, you have kept your promise of redemption. May we show our gratitude and love by obedience to your commandments. *Amen.*

AM: Psalm 93, 96; PM: Psalm 148, 150; Baruch 4:21-29; *Galatians 3:15-22;* Luke 1:67-80 *or* Matthew 1:1-17

Emmanuel

The virgin shall conceive and bear a son,
and they shall name him Emmanuel
which means, 'God is with us.'

Matthew 1:23

It is Christmas Eve! Many years ago those words meant the coming of — Santa Claus. My mother had her hands full with six kids to keep out of trouble and out of the presents piled under the Christmas tree. What was Santa Claus bringing me? Was it what I wanted? How hard it was to go to sleep!

When I had my own family Christmas Eve was still a chaotic time. It was my turn to deal with the stress and tension of last-minute preparations. There was more baking to be done and advance preparations for the big meal the next day. And then it was time to hurry up and get dressed for church.

Later in the evening there were still gifts to wrap, and sometimes something to be secretly assembled. Once we hid a toy chest in our shed and then had a hard time getting it out because the shed's lock had frozen. We were sure the neighbors thought we were burglars! It was usually the wee hours of Christmas morning before I collapsed into bed.

For several years I decorated a "meditation wall" in my church that kept me busy through the morning hours of Christmas Eve, changing the display from Advent to Christmas. One Christmas Eve snowflakes were flying when I began to pack up and leave the church. I barely made it home before a blizzard began that canceled the Christmas Eve services.

Now times have changed. Christmas Eve is usually very quiet for me. I attend the early service at church. Then I head home alone to finish any remaining preparations for my Christmas Day. Christmas carols are usually the only sounds that fill my house now on Christmas Eve.

Yet there is something that rises up inside of me when I wake up; I feel a special excitement knowing it is Christmas Eve. And as I sing "Silent Night" at the end of the church service and later when I place the baby Jesus in the manger before I go to bed, I always know what it is: "To you is born this day in the city of David a Saviour, who is the Messiah, the Lord." (Luke 2:1)

This is what we have waited for with much anticipation all through Advent. Not the birth of just any child, but the birth of our Savior, the Messiah, Jesus Christ our Lord. Over the years that anticipation has only grown for me. And the joy within me rises as the time for celebration draws near.

As midnight approaches, all over the world is hushed, hushed, hushed; indeed the world falls silent, remembering that night so long ago. That silent night, that holy night.

And then Jesus comes into the world, "and they shall name him Emmanuel which means, 'God is with us." And, yes, on this holiest of holy nights, at long last, to a sad and weary world, God is with us. Rejoice!

O heavenly Father, thank you for the gift of your Son, our Savior, Jesus Christ! *Amen.*

Oh, come let us adore him, Christ the Lord.

Psalm 96; Isaiah 9:2-7; Titus 2:11-14; *Luke 2: 1-14 (15-20)*

Christmas

The virgin shall conceive and bear a son,
and they shall name him Emmanuel
which means, 'God is with us.'

Matthew 1:23

Christ
Healer
Redeemer
Incarnation
Savior
Teacher
Messiah
Anointed
Son of God

Oh Come Let Us Adore Him,
Christ the Lord!

December 25   Christmas Day

A Baby Boy

And she gave birth to her firstborn son and wrapped him in bands of cloth, and laid him in a manger, because there was no place for them in the inn.

Luke 2:7

A baby boy! I remember holding that new-born child closely in my arms. I touched his face and hands. He felt so warm. He smelled so good. In spite of the nurses' attempts to "swaddle" him he had managed to work his thumb free so he could suck on it. His first pictures shows him with his eyes tightly closely and both of his little arms pressing snuggly against the sides of his face. What a lot of hair he had!

Mary's experience was different. "She gave birth to her first born son and wrapped him in bands of cloth, and laid him in a manger, because there was no place for them in the inn." (Luke 2:7) The air her new-born baby breathed must have been damp and full of the smell of animals and dirty straw. Perhaps the sound of lowing animals accompanied her as she soothed her son to sleep.

I do believe that Mary did experience that thrill that all new mothers feel when their newborn child is laid in their arms. A new creation! What a gift! What a joy!

God our heavenly Father, thank you for this new creation, for the gift of your Son, our Savior, Jesus Christ. *Amen.*

Psalm 97:
Isaiah 62:6-12; Titus 3:4-7; *Luke 2: (1-7) 8-20*

Monday   St. Stephen, Deacon & Martyr

Why Stone Stephen?

While they were stoning Stephen, he prayed,
'Lord Jesus, receive my spirit.'

Acts 7:69

St. Stephen is considered to be the first martyr of the new church. He was one of seven men the apostles chose to assist with the administration of the early church. "Friends, select from among yourselves seven men of good standing, full of the Spirit and of wisdom, whom we may appoint to this task, while we, for our part, will devote ourselves to prayer and to serving the word." (Act 6:3-4)

Unfortunately, Stephen incurred the wrath of some members of a local synagogue. They secretly instigated some men to say, "'[W]e have heard him speak blasphemous words against Moses and God.' They stirred up the people as well as the elders and the scribes; then they suddenly confronted him, seized him, and brought him before the council." (Acts 7:11-12).

Stephen further angered the synagogue members:

You stiff-necked people, uncircumcised in heart and ears, you are forever opposing the Holy Spirit, just as your ancestors used to do. Which of the prophets did your ancestors not persecute? They killed those who foretold the coming of the Righteous One, and now you have become his betrayers and murderers. You are the ones that received the law as ordained by angels, and yet you have not kept it.

Acts 7:51-53

Accused of breaking the law and of being betrayers and

murderers of Jesus, "they became enraged and ground their teeth at Stephen." (v. 54) Finally, "they covered their ears, and with a loud shout all rushed together against him. Then they dragged him out of the city and began to stone him." (vv.57-58)

In my mind the question forms: "Why stone Stephen?" When good people speak out what they believe is the truth some people just cannot stand to hear it. Rather than accept the fact that someone can think or believe differently, people allow their emotions to lead them to irrational acts. This is not the behavior of a good Christian or a good Jew. These are mindless, senseless, violent acts. And they are sins against God whether committed by a member of any denomination or faith community.

Stephen's martyrdom brings to mind some aspects of the persecution and death of Jesus. He, too, was plotted against and falsely accused. Just as a crowd shouted out against Stephen, a similar crowd in Jerusalem was stirred up to cry out against Jesus, "Crucify him!" Both Jesus and Stephen also pleaded for mercy for their persecutors. Jesus said, "Father, forgive them; for they do not know what they are doing." (Luke 23:34) "While they were stoning Stephen, he prayed, 'Lord Jesus, receive my spirit.' Then he knelt down and cried out in a loud voice, 'Lord, do not hold this sin against them.' When he had said this, he died." (Acts 7:59-60)

When we, too, are filled with rage because someone does not share our beliefs what do we do? How do we react? Do we pick up stones? Do we join the mob? Do we have a choice? Yes. Let us put down our stones. We have already crucified Christ.

Lord Jesus, when our hearts are filled with anger and hate, help us to remember that you commanded us to love our neighbor. All are our brothers and sisters in Christ. *Amen.*

Psalm 31 or 31:1-5; Jeremiah 26:1-9, 12-15;
Acts 6:8-7:2a, 51c-60; Matthew 23:34-39

70

Tuesday   St. John, Apostle and Evangelist

Our Joy May Be Complete

We declare to you what we have seen and heard so that you also may have fellowship with us; and truly our fellowship is with the Father and with his Son Jesus Christ. We are writing these things so that our joy may be complete.

1 John 1:1-4

We do not know what it was like to walk on the earth with Jesus. We were not privileged to hear personally Jesus tell a parable or preach a sermon. We were not present at his crucifixion; we did not share in the joyous news of his resurrection. Personal witness is powerful but sometimes we must rely on the word of others to describe "what we have seen with our eyes, what we have looked at and touched with our hands." (1 John 1:1) John and the other authors of the New Testament are such messengers to us.

Today in our world of instant communication we are inundated with "news" Sometimes this news is "eyewitness" and sometimes it is a link to a website or a message shared from another. No matter what the source of information people want to share what they have seen and heard.

In the same way John wanted to relate to others what he had experienced firsthand. He also wanted to convey how what both what was shown and what was revealed to him and to the other apostles not only changed their lives but could change the lives of all people. "We have seen it and testify to it, and declare to you the eternal life that was with the Father and was revealed to us." (v.2) This is the "good news" of salvation for all mankind.

71

John wanted others to join in the fellowship that he found with God and with Jesus Christ. "We are writing these things so that our joy may be complete." (v.3) For John completeness came from what had been revealed to him as well as the opportunity to share that with others. "This is the message we have heard from him and proclaim to you, that God is light and in him there is no darkness at all." (v.5) Fellowship is created by the bond of shared knowledge and acceptance of the message. "If we walk in the light of God we have fellowship with one another, and the blood of Jesus his Son cleanses us from all sin." (v.7)

What greater joy could there have been than to be able to tell people that Jesus Christ was the Messiah and that by his atoning sacrifice we are saved from sin and have the hope of eternal life? "If we confess our sins, he who is faithful and just will forgive us our sins and cleanse us from all unrighteousness." (9) John wanted to share that good news.

John was excited about the message he had to share. He was like the little boy tugging on his mother's sleeve, anxious to tell his latest news. John's message is like the latest email we receive, "Did you hear…?" Today John would be sending text messages, "tweeting" everyone, and posting all about the good news on Facebook. He would be hoping to be "friended" by many people.

John's not here. We are. We have the opportunity to use our favorite forms of communication to share the same information about the forgiveness of sins that John was so eager to share. We also seek fellowship in the knowledge and love of Jesus Christ. Why not share the good news?

Jesus, help us to follow the example of John, using every form of communication to spread the good news of your saving grace. *Amen.*

Psalm 92 or 92:1-4, 11-14;
Exodus 33:18-23; *1 John 1:1-9;* John 21:9b-24

Wednesday   The Holy Innocents

Rachel is weeping for her children

A voice is heard in Ramah,
  lamentation and bitter weeping.
Rachel is weeping for her children;
  she refuses to be comforted for her children,
  because they are no more.

Jeremiah 31:15

The story of the "Holy Innocents" is a sad one. King Herod of Judea was anxious when he heard of the prophecy of a "king of the Jews:" "for from you shall come a ruler/ who is to shepherd my people Israel." (Matthew 2:6) Fearful of a powerful leader arising in Israel Herod asked the Wise Men to report Jesus' location to him. When the wise men foiled King Herod's plan to find out the location of the Christ child, "he sent and killed all the children in and around Bethlehem who were two years old or under, according to the time that he had learned from the wise men." (v. 16). Jesus was spared "because an angel of the Lord appeared to Joseph in a dream and said, 'Get up, take the child and his mother, and flee to Egypt, and remain there until I tell you; for Herod is about to search for the child, to destroy him.'" (v.13). The result was that many innocent children were slaughtered.

Holy and innocent —and dead. This is one of those bible stories that strikes hard at a mother's heart. "Rachel is weeping for her children; she refuses to be comforted for her children, because they are no more." (Jeremiah 31:15) Any mother reading this can feel the grief at the loss of her child. Why did all these mothers have to sacrifice their babies?

The slaughter of babies recalls the story of Moses and

73

others in the Old Testament. Matthew explained the connection to Egypt: "This was to fulfil what had been spoken by the Lord through the prophet, 'Out of Egypt I have called my son.'" (Matthew 2:15) This story also foreshadows Jesus' encounters with the Roman rulers and shows Rome's dominance over the Jewish people. And the mothers' grief also foreshadows Mary's grief as she watched her own son tortured and crucified.

Mary and Joseph must have been terrified. Yes, they had been told that the child was the Messiah, the Son of God, but they had received no advance warning that he would be the target of Roman authorities. The ultimate purpose of this relocation according to Matthew was to fulfill a prophetic saying about the Messiah: "'He will be called a Nazorean.'" (Matthew 2:23) A lot of suffering was caused needlessly. Mary and Joseph could have decided to make their home in a different place. And that would not have been so extraordinary considering the issues relating to the child's conception.

None of these explanations about fulfillment of prophecies or about a show of power seem to offer a sufficient reason for the murder of innocent children. Do we then look to God for the answer? God is certainly the one in charge. God's angels carried his messages and he controlled the story.

Am I questioning God's motive? No, not his motive because I do not know what it is. Blame my questioning on a mother's heart. God, why did those innocent little babies have to die?

Merciful God, forgive this mother's grieving heart. I know you hold those innocent babies in your bosom. *Amen.*

Psalm 124;
Jeremiah 31:15-17; Revelation 21:1-7; Matthew 2:13-18

There was a Wedding in Cana

There was a wedding in Cana of Galilee, and the mother of Jesus was there. Jesus and his disciples had also been invited to the wedding.

John 2:1-2

This story starts out like a social column in the newspaper, the opening of an entertainment news program or the headline of an online entertainment article. "There was a wedding in Cana of Galilee."(John 2:1) ("Wedding of the Year!") The mother of Jesus was there. (v.1) ("Mary looked divine in her new robes.") "Jesus and his disciples had also been invited to the wedding." (v.2) ("Jesus was there with a new crowd; some of them looked a bit out of place.") ("We have the exclusive interview.")

This wedding was probably not really prominent enough to make the "A" list but it gives a brief glimpse into the life of Jesus on the threshold of his ministry. I can see Mary, huddled with her friends, talking about the wedding party and sharing favorite recipes. Joseph is not mentioned so the assumption would be that he had already died. Jesus and his disciples were also there. Perhaps Jesus was introducing his new friends to family members, the wedding party, and others. It seems familiar and comforting that Jesus and his mother took part in the social events of the community.

Today many people host festive events during the holiday season. Some people have Christmas parties; others have New Year's celebrations or even football bowl "watch" parties. Families often have Christmas dinners or other gatherings with family members. Wedding are not uncommon this time of year. I usually host a holiday get-together with friends while on vacation between Christmas Eve and New Year's Day. So the story of the wedding in Cana fits right in here.

The interaction between Jesus and his mother at the wedding is interesting. Mary noted that the wine had run out: "She says to Jesus: 'They have no wine.' And Jesus said to her, 'Woman, what concern is that to you and to me? My hour has not yet come.'" (3-4) Jesus' response does not seem meant to be disrespectful; rather, it is as if he wants to pick the time and place to "go public." But it seems the "hour" was chosen for him, just as he had no control over the hour of his death.

The "miracle," the changing of water into wine, did not happen accompanied by fanfare or even a prayer. It just happened. The greater significance lies in its foreshadowing of the Last Supper when the wine becomes the blood of Jesus; blood shed for us all.

It is interesting that this story appears in the Gospel of John, the gospel far less focused on the miracles and parables of Jesus than the synoptic gospels. In fact, this story is not in any of the other gospels. The importance to John is undoubtedly that the events that are said to have occurred during the wedding are considered to be Jesus' first miracle (John calls them "signs"). John concluded the story by saying that there, for the first time, Jesus "revealed his glory; and his disciples believed in him." (11) This first miracle of Jesus revealed who he was and provided an opportunity for his disciples to express their belief in him.

Blessed Jesus, signs of your saving grace are all around us. We need only to open our eyes and ears to perceive you at work in the world around us. *Amen.*

AM: Psalm 18:1-20. PM: Psalm 18:21-50;
2 Samuel 23:13-17b; 2 John 1:13; *John 2:1-11*

Friday   Week of Christmas

The Man Believed

Then Jesus said to him, 'Unless you see signs and wonders you will not believe.' The official said to him, 'Sir, come down before my little boy dies.' Jesus said to him, 'Go; your son will live.' The man believed the word that Jesus spoke to him and started on his way.

John 4:48-50

"Unless you see signs and wonders you will not believe." (John 4:48) I take this statement as a challenge from Jesus to the Roman official. The man's response is to keep begging Jesus for his help. After Jesus says to the official: "'Go; your son will live.' The man believed the word that Jesus spoke to him and started on his way." (v.50) "The man believed." The account does not say what he believed or how much he believed, but he did believe enough to start back home to check on his child.

When presented with the reality that his son was alive, "he asked them the hour when he began to recover, and they said to him, 'Yesterday at one in the afternoon the fever left him.'" The father realized that this was the hour when Jesus had said to him. "Your son will live." (v.52-53) Was this lingering doubt that needed a sign or was this faith being confirmed?

John reiterates this point with the story of Thomas the Apostle. Thomas is not present when Jesus first appears to the disciples. He does not believe their story of the risen Christ. "Unless I see the mark of the nails in his hands, and put my finger in the mark of the nails and my hand in his side, I will not believe." (John 20:25) When Jesus again stood in their midst, this time with Thomas present, he said to Thomas, "Put your finger here and see my hands. Reach out your hand and put it in

77

my side. Do not doubt but believe.' Thomas answered him, 'My Lord and my God!" Jesus then said to him, "Have you believed because you have seen me? Blessed are those who have not seen and yet have come to believe." (John 20:27-29)

Recently I went through a period of doubt and uncertainty. I was living under the shadow of the possibility that I had thyroid cancer. Shortly after I received this news I spent some time in prayer over this at my church. As I was praying I felt a great sense of calm and peacefulness descending upon me. I believed I would be healed and whole. Still that did not remove all of my anxiety as I underwent further tests, and especially as I awaited the results of those tests.

My prayer was for healing, but also that God's will for me be done. As I did not know if that healing would be to find that the nodule was benign or that I would soon find myself with God, I reacted in a very human way. I worried. And I said to God more than once, "I believe; forgive my unbelief."

So maybe it's not really "signs and wonders" that we need, but confirmation. We get the results of our tests, we see our son is alive, we place our fingers in Jesus' wounds and then we can move on with greater confidence in our growing faith. I believe that God understands this about human nature. The story ends with the strengthening of the official's faith: "so he himself believed, along with his whole household." (John 4:54). Having faith is like taking a journey not knowing the destination before you get there. It is a life-long process.

Jesus, even though we believe in you with all our hearts, we have times of doubt and weakness. Strengthen our faith in you, O Lord. *Amen.*

AM: Psalm 20, 21:1-7(8-14); PM: Psalm 23, 27;
1Kings 17:17-24; 3 John 1-15; ***John 4:46-54***

Saturday   Eve of Holy Name

A Very Present Help in Trouble

God is our refuge and strength, a very present help in
   trouble.
Therefore we will not fear, though the earth should change,
   though the mountains shake in the heart of the sea;
though its waters roar and foam,
   though the mountains tremble with its tumult.

Psalm 46

New Year's Eve is a traditional time to look back on the
past year. This year seems to have been especially filled with
catastrophic events and crises. Extreme weather events have
occurred across the globe. A tornado wiped out one third of
the city of Joplin, Missouri and killed over 150 people. Record
lows and highs have been set. Other natural phenomena such
as earthquakes, tsunamis and floods have taken their toll. An
earthquake and tsunami devastated a large portion of Japan.
Major floods have plagued areas of Australia, China, and the
United States.

Across the world, there has been plenty of political and
financial upheaval as well. Dictators in Tunisia, Libya and Egypt
have been toppled. Many countries such as Greece and Ireland
face difficult financial times.

But is there any such thing as a "normal" or "quiet" year?
Yes, some years seem to be extreme in perspective but there
are always natural disasters and conflicts occurring someplace
across the globe. The world is a place of constant change; it is
no paradise.

Our lives are like that, too. We have years when crises seem

79

to come one right on top of another. Other times life seems to be going along rather smoothly. But no life is completely void of worries and problems.

Who do we turn to when the going gets rough? We have family and we have friends. And we have so much more in the God who created us, his Son who redeemed us, and his Spirit who guides us daily. Where is God in all of this? He is right there with us. He is "our refuge and our strength."

This year is ending. It is time to look forward. What will next year bring? We do not know what earthly events might occur. We cannot say what will happen in our own lives, but we do know that God is ever present. Therefore "we will not fear," but move forward confidently, putting our faith and trust in God.

God, you are always present in our lives; Jesus, our brother, walks by our sides. As we begin a new year we renew our commitment to live a new life in Christ, putting our whole faith and trust in you, O Lord our God. *Amen.*

Psalm 46, 48
1 Kings 3:5-14; James 4:13-17; 5:7-11; John 5:1-15

Christmas 1

She will bear a son,
and you are to name him Jesus,
for he will save his people from their sins.

Matthew 1:21

Sunday   (First Sunday after Christmas)

The Holy Name of Jesus

She will bear a son,
and you are to name him Jesus,
for he will save his people from their sins.

Matthew 1:21

According to the liturgical calendar of the Episcopal Church we celebrate the holy name of Jesus on January 1st. How wonderful that we begin the new year with a celebration of the name that was the beginning of our new life. Jesus is our Lord and our God from the first day to the last.

How did Jesus get his name? In the Gospel of Luke the angel Gabriel told Mary, "you will conceive in your womb and bear a son, and you will name him Jesus." (Luke 1:31). According to the gospel of Matthew, when Joseph found out at that Mary was pregnant before they had married he intended to make some private arrangements to divorce her. However, an angel appeared to Joseph in a dream and told him, "do not be afraid to take Mary as your wife, for the child conceived in her is from the Holy Spirit. She will bear a son, and you are to name him Jesus, for he will save his people from their sins." (Matthew 1:20-21.) Jesus, "he who saves"; our Savior.

Jesus, the holiest of names, was given to him by his heavenly Father. "Therefore God also highly exalted him and gave him the name that is above every name." (2:9) Jesus is the one name that should always be on the tip of our tongues and most of all it should be enthroned in our hearts. "At the name of Jesus every knee should bend, in heaven and on earth and under the earth,

83

and every tongue should confess that Jesus Christ is Lord, to the glory of God the Father." (Philippians 2:10-11)

The name of Jesus is invoked in prayer and in praise by all who believe in him. Popular movements, societies, and seminars carry the name of Jesus. The "Jesus Prayer": "Lord Jesus Christ, Son Of God, have mercy upon me, a sinner." is used by various churches, groups and individuals.

Words from a favorite hymn of mine express the power and the glory of the name of Jesus:

> *At the Name of Jesus*
> *every knee shall bow,*
> *every tongue confess him*
> *King of glory now;*
> *'tis the Father's pleasure*
> *we should call him Lord,*
> *who from the beginning*
> *was the mighty Word.*
>
> *Name him, brothers, name him,*
> *with love as strong as death,*
> *but with awe and wonder*
> *and with bated breath;*
> *he is God the Savior,*
> *he is Christ the Lord,*
> *ever to be worshiped,*
> *trusted, and adored.*

Caroline M. Noel (1817-1877), 1870

Jesus, you are the Lord of our lives. We praise and bless your holy name. *Amen.*

AM Psalm 103; PM: Psalm 148
Isaiah 62:1-5, 10-12; Revelation 19:11-16; *Matthew 1:18-25*

Monday   Week of 1st Sunday after Christmas

A Life Worthy

Lead a life worthy of the calling to which you have been called, with all humility and gentleness, with patience, bearing with one another in love, making every effort to maintain the unity of the Spirit in the bond of peace.

Ephesians 4:1-3

How do we lead a life worthy of being called Christians? Paul begins the fourth chapter of his letter to the Ephesians by begging them to "lead a life worthy of the calling to which you have been called." (Ephesians 4:1). Paul's version of New Year's resolutions for the Ephesians is a tall order. He asks them to practice humility, gentleness and patience. Patience would probably be something good to put at the top of our list. For me it is both patience with others, and patience with myself.

Next on Paul's list is "bearing with one another in love." That certainly requires more patience along with tolerance and acceptance. Paul also mentions humility, and add to that something that can be tough to swallow —pride. Updating Paul's list one also might want to include reminders about attitude and pettiness. Treating everyone with loving kindness can forge bonds of peace within a community. Individuals strive to lead virtuous lives that bring them into communion with other believers and together they build up each other and they build up the Body of Christ.

Paul maintains that unity is essential to the body of Christ: "There is one body and one Spirit, just as you were called to the one hope of your calling, one Lord, one faith, one baptism, one God and Father of all, who is above all and through all and in

85

all." (4-6) Although individual members of the community are called to different ministries, "some would be apostles, some prophets, some evangelists, some pastors and teachers," (v.11) all must work for the common good and to build up the body of Christ. This spirit of unity is the foundation for the maturation of the people as a community of believers. The work of building up the body continues "until all of us come to the unity of the faith and of the knowledge of the Son of God, to maturity, to the measure of the full stature of Christ." (v.13-14).

This work of building up of the Body of Christ continues today. As new members are added they must come to understand the importance of leading lives that reflect Christian values. Being a part of a Christian community aids members in the task of maturing in the faith and the knowledge and love of God.

We, as Christians, are called to practice the same virtues as the Ephesians. Our New Year's Resolution list should mirror the list that Paul had for the Ephesians. When we put these resolutions into practice we will reflect the teachings of Jesus and become members of the body of Christ. In our faith communities and in the communities of the world we will be living examples of what it means to be a Christian. We will be leading lives worthy of our calling as Christians.

None of this is easy to do. Leading such a life requires hard work on our part. It requires support of and support from others. It requires grace from God and most of all it requires faith in Jesus Christ.

Lord, leading a life worthy of the name Christian can only be accomplished with your grace and blessings to sustain us and support us. *Amen.*

AM: Psalm 34; PM: Psalm 33
1 Kings 19:1-8; *Ephesians* 4:1-16; John 6:1-14

Tuesday   Week of 1st Sunday after Christmas

Sing to God, Sing Praises to his Name;

Sing to God, sing praises to his name;
*   lift up a song to him who rides upon the clouds—*
his name is the Lord—
*   be exultant before him.*

Psalm 68:4

During Advent and the Christmas Season we decorate our houses, we give presents to one another and we celebrate the seasons. We decorate our churches also, lovingly placing the crèche in front of our altars, hanging wreaths and garland. We sing beautiful Christmas carols. These are all ways we celebrate the coming of Christ into the world at Christmas time.

Now it is almost time to take down the decorations and the tree. That is unless you already threw out your tree with the leftover turkey. The Christmas season does not end until Epiphany.

Life goes on. Back to school; back to work. All those Christmas bills are coming due. It seems like we all too quickly forget the reason for the Christmas season.

Praise to God and thanksgiving for all he has done for us is not just for the holy season of Christmas. It should be part of our lives daily. "Our God is a God of salvation." (Psalm 68:20) God has given us a Messiah. He has delivered his people from sin and death. God is worthy of our thanks and praise at all times and in all places. "Sing to God, sing praises to his name; lift up a song to him who rides upon the clouds—his name is the Lord —be exultant before him." (Psalm 68:4)

It is all too easy to put Jesus up on the shelf with the Christmas decorations. Yes, we celebrate the coming of the Magi with their gifts but then the joy of Jesus often fades from our lives. He remains in the background until at least Palm Sunday, when we again greet him with hosannas and hymns of praise. Then do we suddenly remember that Jesus came to save us from our sins?

God's presence is not a one-day event. "Blessed be the Lord, who daily bears us up; God is our salvation." (Psalm 68:19) Jesus is with us every day of our lives, not just at Christmas. His saving grace supports us. His Spirit is with us to listen to our pleas and our prayers.

Do not just sink into the doldrums of winter and forget that the God who created you is recreating you and the world around you every day. Greet him daily with praise and thanksgiving; offer prayers and hymns of praise at worship services; joyfully spread the good news of Jesus Christ through love of family, friend and neighbor.

Always and everywhere: "let the righteous be joyful; let them exult before God; let them be jubilant with joy." (Psalm 68:3). Carry forth the joy of the Christmas season. Keep Christmas in your hearts all year.

Loving God, you are worthy of all praise and adoration. May our hearts always be filled love for you as we sing praises to your holy name. *Amen.*

AM*: Psalm 68*; PM: Psalm 72;
1 Kings 19:19:9-18; Ephesians 4:17-32; John 6:15-27

Wednesday   Week of 1ˢᵗ Sunday after Christmas

What do Those Stones Mean to You?

When your children ask in time to come, "What do those stones mean to you?" then you shall tell them that the waters of the Jordan were cut off in front of the ark of the covenant of the LORD.

Joshua 4:6-7

Judaism, Christianity and other religions have monuments or memorials that testify to events of importance in their history. This memorial is a rather interesting one —twelve stones taken from the riverbed of the Jordan. God called for the establishment of this memorial of the dry crossing of the Jordan River. "Pass on before the ark of the Lord your God into the middle of the Jordan, and each of you take up a stone on his shoulder, one for each of the tribes of the Israelites, so that this may be a sign among you." (Joshua 4:5-6) "The stones were then taken to the place where the Israelites camped for the night. When future generations would ask, 'What do those stones mean to you?' then you shall tell them that the waters of the Jordan were cut off in front of the ark of the covenant of the LORD. When it crossed over the Jordan, the waters of the Jordan were cut off." (Joshua 4:6-7) Thus a memorial to this miraculous event was established.

Other religious sites of historic importance can be found around the world. Jerusalem is a holy city claimed by three religions: Judaism, Christianity and Islam. The Temple Mount has ties to both Judaism and Islam. The "Wailing Wall" in Old Jerusalem is part of the remnants of the Jewish Temple.

The Church of the Nativity in Bethlehem is built over a cave that is considered to be the traditional birthplace of Jesus. The

Church of the Holy Sepulchre in Jerusalem is said to be the site of Golgotha, the location of Jesus' crucifixion. It is also Christ's traditional burial site.

Al-Masjid al-Harām, "The Sacred Mosque" is located in the city of Mecca. It contains the Kaaba, the place where all Muslims turn for daily prayers and is considered to be Islam's holiest place. All able-bodied Muslims are required by their religion to make a pilgrimage to this site.

When people visit these holy places they are reminded of the significance of the place to their religion and how that affects their own beliefs. In our communities we build churches, temples and mosques as our own places of worship. If we have been a long-time member of a particular faith community we attach significance to particular items within our places of worship. Members of our own faith community made many items in our church, including our altar and columbarium. We remember these people and their contribution to our church. The things they have made show us ways God is working in our faith community just as he was at work in the parting of the Jordan so the Ark of the Lord could pass.

We have the opportunity to pass along the history and memories associated with our religious objects to our children, to visitors and to others who worship there after us. When people ask about them we share our stories just as the ancient Israelites had the opportunity to do: "When your children ask in time to come, 'What do those stones mean to you?'" (Joshua 4:6).

Heavenly Father, your hand is always at work in our communities and in our lives. Let us speak with pride of the work you have called us to do and give thanks for your hand in it. *Amen.*

AM: Psalm 85, 87; PM: Psalm 89:1-29
Joshua 3:14—4:7; Eph. 5:1-20; John 9:1-12, 35-38

Thursday   Week of 1st Sunday after Christmas

Out of the Belly of Sheol I Cried

I called to the Lord out of my distress,
and he answered me;
out of the belly of Sheol I cried,
and you heard my voice.

Jonah 2: 2

Jonah was called by God to prophesy to the people of Nineveh. Apparently Jonah was not too keen on being a messenger of doom; he took off in the opposite direction. Jonah got himself in a lot of trouble by trying to get "away from the presence of the Lord" (Jonah 1:3). When he tried to escape by sea God responded. "The Lord hurled a great wind upon the sea, and such a mighty storm came upon the sea that the ship threatened to break up." (Jonah 1:4) Eventually Jonah's shipmates threw him overboard to appease his god. In fact it was Jonah's idea. "He said to them, 'Pick me up and throw me into the sea; then the sea will quieten down for you; for I know it is because of me that this great storm has come upon you.'" (Jonah 1:12)

Well, Jonah was right about that. As soon as he was pitched overboard "the sea ceased from its raging." (Jonah 1:15). So God saved the men on the ship and God saved Jonah. "The Lord provided a large fish to swallow up Jonah." (Jonah 1:17b) And God left Jonah in the belly of that fish for three days. Maybe that was to give him time to think about his actions?

What did Jonah do? He started praying. But some parts of Jonah's prayer do not ring quite true. Jonah said Lord, "*You* [emphasis added] cast me into the deep, into the heart of the seas, and the flood surrounded me; all your waves and your billows

91

passed over me" (Jonah 2:3) Now wait a minute. Whose idea was it that the men pitch Jonah into the sea? It was Jonah's idea, not God's, although he was probably about ready to do so anyway. And then Jonah said, "I am driven away from your sight; how shall I look again upon your holy temple?" (Jonah 2:4). Jonah was the one who took off; God did not drive him away.

Jonah said: "Out of the belly of Sheol [hell] I cried." (Jonah 2:2) Well, the hell was of his own making. He made a decision not to follow the will of the Lord, he ran away, and he nearly paid with his life for his actions. God, who is merciful, saved him anyway, in spite of his willful disobedience. "I called to the Lord out of my distress, and he answered me." (Jonah 2:2) But maybe Jonah did not get quite the answer he was expecting. I doubt he was expecting that God would have a fish swallow him. So now he is praying. "But I with the voice of thanksgiving will sacrifice to you; what I have vowed I will pay. Deliverance belongs to the Lord!" (Jonah 2:9) He means *real* deliverance this time.

The rest of Jonah's story tells more about his attitude towards God's mercy but it is obvious from this small part that Jonah thinks God should see things his way. Jonah would have better served God and Nineveh from the beginning by openly sharing his feelings with the Lord and praying for help to overcome his own selfishness. We often want God to do things our way, but God in his divine wisdom follows his plans, not ours.

Loving and merciful God, we are blessed that you save us from ourselves. Teach us to follow your will with loving and obedient hearts. *Amen.*

AM: Psalm 2, 110:1-5(6-7);
Jonah 2:2-9; Ephesians 6:10-20; John 11:17-27, 38-44

Epiphany

Where is the child who has been born king of the Jews? For we observed his star at its rising, and have come to pay him homage.

Matthew 2:2

Friday   Epiphany

Our Gifts

Ascribe to the LORD the glory due his name;
bring an offering, and come into his courts.

Psalm 96:8

"In the time of King Herod, after Jesus was born in Bethlehem of Judea, wise men from the East came to Jerusalem." Matthew 2:1) "The wise men were searching for the king of the Jews. They asked Herod, 'Where is the child who has been born king of the Jews? For we observed his star at its rising, and have come to pay him homage.'" (Matthew 2:2). The Bible tells us the Magi brought precious gifts to give the Christ Child: "opening their treasure-chests, they offered him gifts of gold, frankincense, and myrrh." (Matthew 2:11).

"Ascribe to the LORD the glory due his name; bring an offering, and come into his courts." (Psalm 96:8) Jesus had no court; he was only a tiny baby in a manger. But God had revealed the kingship of Christ to the wise men and they came to pay him homage and give him gifts — gifts to honor an earthly king. We know that Jesus' court is a heavenly one where we will some day present the gift of our lives.

Here and now on earth we do have gifts we can give. Sometimes we have to think about what kind of gifts we really have to give and what they can mean to others and to God. Around pledge time at church we usually hear that we have "time, talent, and treasure" to give to the church. We know that the church needs whatever financial assistance we can give to pay for salaries, maintenance, programs etc. Churches and other faith communities also need funds to support outreach. Through these kinds of programs we assist those in need in our community. We may also choose to support other charities outside of the church.

How do you give time? It may sound easy to say, "sign up to help with _____," but it may not be that easy to do. Giving time involves sacrifice, just like giving money. You may have to give up a favorite TV show or get up earlier on Saturday.

It may be that figuring out to how to give "talent" is the hardest of all. Sometimes you can readily identify that you have a particular talent like cooking or working on cars. However you may not know of any talent that you think will be useful to your church or to a charitable organization. But God does; listen to his Spirit. Trying, experimenting, and even failing are ways to find out. And don't give up. You do have gifts you can share with others.

Everything you do in the name of Jesus is an offering to God. God spared nothing for us, not even his only son. We may not even give any thought to how we are blessed by both our giving and our receiving. "Sing to the Lord, bless his name; tell of his salvation from day to day. Declare his glory among the nations, his marvellous works among all the peoples." (Psalm 96:2-3) What can we do to further God's work on earth? What can we give back to God, blessed as we are by all that God has given us?

Dear God, help us to find our true gifts so that we may offer them to you and use them for your glory. *Amen.*

AM Psalm 46, 97; PM: *Psalm 96*, 100;
Isaiah 49:1-7; Revelation 21:22-27; Matthew 12:14-21

ANNUNCIATION   INCARNATION   MANIFESTATION

ANNUNCIATION	INCARNATION	MANIFESTATION
*Annunci**A**tion*	***C**hrist*	***E**ast*
*House of **D**avid*	**H**oly	*Worshi**P***
***V**isitation*	*Ado**R**ation*	*G**I**fts*
*Pr**E**paration*	**I**ncarnation	*Jose**P**h*
*Repenta**N**ce*	*Je**S**us*	**H**erod
*John **T**he Baptist*	*Na**T**ivity*	*St**A**r*
	Mary	*Wise Me**N***
	Angels	*Eg**Y**pt*
	*Shepherd**S***	

97

About the Author

Diane Zike has a B. A. in English Literature from the City College of the City University of New York and holds a Master of Arts Degree (Ministry and Culture) from Phillips Theological Seminary in Tulsa, Oklahoma. She received her initial training in pastoral care while assisting in the Tulsa Episcopal Chaplaincy program. Diane completed a unit of Clinical Pastoral Education at Hillcrest Medical Center in Tulsa.

Diane brings a variety of life experiences to the writing of meditations. She was the chaplain and director for Interfaith AIDS Ministries in Tulsa for ten years. Diane served on the Diocesan AIDS Commission of the Episcopal Diocese of Oklahoma. She also worked in hospice and served on a regional advisory board for the Oklahoma Department of Mental Health. Diane has led workshops on hospital visitation, AIDS and death and dying issues and has written brochures and other materials on these topics.

Diane is a member of St. Peter's Episcopal Church in Tulsa where she provides lay Eucharistic visitation and leads a Wednesday Compline Service.

Diane is currently working on a book of poems and prayers, and she has two Lenten Meditation books planned for 2012.

Acknowledgements

Special thanks to Darlene A. Cypser for her setup, layout, proofing and promotion work. Thank you to Linda Thomas for taking the time to proof each meditation. Thanks always to all my friends and family for their love and support.

56544770R00059